PITCH TO WIN

I have had the privilege to witness first-hand how David's powerful coaching has helped numerous startups, professionals and innovation leaders improve their pitch. *Pitch to Win* brings the best of his tools, experience and lessons learned, together in one practical and actionable book.
— **Ilja Linnemeier, Head of Digital, PwC.**

A masterful how-to manual for engaging people in what you want them to do. Beckett's focus on high-intensity, high-payoff presentations, has produced a wealth of great coaching here for all who would like to influence anyone else, about anything. Though I've done presentations for years, it's given me some real gems I'll use right away!
— **David Allen, author of the international bestseller,** *Getting Things Done: The Art of Stress-Free Productivity.*

It's not only the big ideas that benefit from David's work. You'll learn valuable new ways of thinking and communicating for impact, and have fun along the way. Highly recommended.
— **Arne-Cristian van der Tang, Chief HR Officer TomTom.**

David was a wonderful coach when I pitched my first startup ComfyLight. I am glad David put all his key points into this book, to help everyone get their story from good to great. Our pitch raised some million euros and David certainly had a part in that development.
— **Stefanie Turber, founder ComfyLight.**

I've seen David transform ordinary presenters into fantastic pitchers. Follow the steps in *Pitch to Win* and you'll have a great shot at pitching successfully for the resources you need to make your innovation ideas a success.
— **Patrick de Zeeuw, cofounder Startupbootcamp.**

This book is an excellent practical toolkit. David is the best pitch coach in the world and provides you with tips and tricks to give your ideas the best possible voice and set yourself up for a winner. Guaranteed success.
— **Michael Dooijes, Managing Director Startupbootcamp FinTech & CyberSecurity, Amsterdam & Frankfurt.**

Pitch to Win gives you all the ingredients to deliver impactful pitches. Whether you are fundraising, giving a management team presentation or pitching your product or service, this book will provide all practicalities needed to nail the pitch and walk away smiling.
— **Frank Appeldoorn, Venture Capital specialist, Arches Capital.**

David is quite simply the Pitch-Maestro. We've worked with him on a wide variety of projects during our meetings, all of which involve culturally diverse audiences from dozens of countries. Whether he's delivering inspirational keynotes, masterfully moderating interactive breakouts, designing innovative and experiential workshops, or delivering personalised training for ICCA's young professionals, to competitively pitch their education session ideas for our next year's Congress. He always delivers beyond expectations. And now he's distilled all of his conceptual and practical knowledge into this one handy package! Of course it doesn't beat the live experience, but if you want to boost your personal impact in front of any audience, it's a great start.
— **Martin Sirk, CEO ICCA, International Congress and Convention Association.**

Pitching is not just for startups. With staff presenting our foundation's story around the world, we need to make sure they can do so in the best way, and David Beckett's training helped us immeasurably. Even if you're an accomplished public speaker, you will improve with his insights.
— **David Campbell, Director of Communications and Engagement, World Press Photo Foundation**

DAVID BECKETT

PITCH TO WIN

THE TOOLS THAT HELP STARTUPS AND CORPORATE INNOVATION TEAMS
SCRIPT, DESIGN, AND DELIVER WINNING PITCHES

VAKMEDIANET

Cover design and book design: Douwe Hoendervanger grafisch ontwerp [bno],
www.douwehoendervanger.nl
Slides design: Robin Dohmen, Elvina Yuliana, owow.io
Pitch Canvas® icons: Birgit Smit, birgitsmit.com
Author portraits: Joost van Manen, joostvanmanen.com
Editor: Sheila Schenkel, fedb.co
Corrections: Dorseda de Block

© 2018 Vakmedianet, Deventer, the Netherlands and David Beckett
Published by Vakmedianet, Deventer

www.vakmedianet.nl
www.managementimpact.nl
pitchtowin.com
www.best3minutes.com

ISBN 978 94 6276 245 9
Audio book 978 94 6276 263 3

TABLE OF CONTENTS

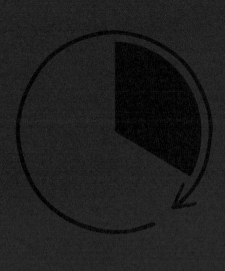

SCRIPT.
page 33

9

DESIGN.

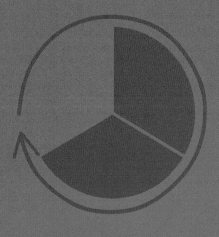

● page 109

DELIVER.

● page 155

14

FOREWORD BY PATRICK DE ZEEUW

I first met David in Summer 2013 at an event we ran at Startupbootcamp called 'Pitch for Coffee!' It was one way to scout for startups in those days, and we gave entrepreneurs five minutes to pitch for us in exchange for a coffee. It worked pretty well, and we found a few great teams.

David didn't have a startup, but rather pitched himself as a mentor for the Startupbootcamp program. He gave an okay pitch! And he was clearly passionate about helping people get their story across. For me it was a no-brainer to bring David on board as lead coach, to help the startup teams in our programs create their stories in a clear and passionate way.

As they grow their disruptive ideas into companies, both startups and corporate innovation teams pitch constantly. It doesn't matter whether you want to raise money from investors, or convince the Board you need time and resources. A short, sharp and persuasive pitch is an essential tool in the team's armoury.

Pitching is an integral part of what entrepreneurs learn at Startupbootcamp. Getting the message across professionally, with maximum impact and passion in a short time, is, I believe, one of the key skills of any startup founder. If you are not able to explain very clearly the problem you are solving, why this problem really matters to you and why you are so passionate about solving it, then your chances of building a successful company decrease big time.

You will not be able to attract the right team members to grow your team or inspire investors to have a conversation with you. Also, it will be harder to attract customers, who are naturally your lifeline.

In the US, presenting and pitching is something you grow up with. In most other countries around the globe, the majority need to be coached on how to pitch.

Increasingly, pitching is becoming important at larger companies too, as

15

major corporates set up innovation teams to develop their future businesses. At Innoleaps, we help large companies implement lean startup tactics and help them grow innovations as well as develop new business models fast and furiously. The founders of these *corporate startups* have many of the same challenges as founders of startups: convincing their stakeholders to invest, attracting the right team members and bringing paying customers onboard.

16

Over the last few years, David has worked with us and many other clients to build up his knowledge and expertise of pitching. He's spent thousands of hours joining events, meeting investors and working with pitchers to identify what helps them grow their skills, as well as create exercises for them to test their stories.

As a result, David gives entrepreneurs practical tools that are easy for them to put into practice, and I've seen him transform ordinary presenters into fantastic pitchers. Those tools are shared openly and generously in this book, and I know that he is totally driven to help his clients shine.

Follow the steps of *Pitch to Win* and you'll have a great shot at pitching successfully for the resources you need to make your innovation idea a success.

Patrick de Zeeuw is a serial entrepreneur and co-founder of one of the world's leading startup accelerators, Startupbootcamp. He is also co-founder of the Corporate Innovation and acceleration house Innoleaps and The Talent Institute, the accelerator for talent. Patrick is a shareholder in over 600 global startups.

Hi,

MY NAME IS DAVID BECKETT. I'M A PITCH COACH AND I BELIEVE GREAT IDEAS NEED A VOICE.

IT STARTED **WITH A PITCH**

0.1 **INTRODUCTION**

My first boss was Lance Miller. It was 1992, and I had just started working at Canon.

Yes, this is me, back in those early days – and the photograph is in black and white because that tie was not a pretty sight....

Lance had worked in advertising for 20 years, and was the best pitcher I'd ever seen: creating a clear story, with immaculately designed slides, presented with utter certainty and passion. Lance could make a mangy mouse look like a well-groomed elephant (and still can today).

In my first weeks in the company, Lance forced me to learn how to pitch persuasively. Visitors to the office? 'Go and tell the story, Beckett!' Exhibition? 'Tell that story one hundred times.' I joined a series of presentation trainings, and watched every move Lance made in every pitch, learning which details made the difference.

This became the most powerful skill I acquired during 16 years at Canon, during which I progressed through all levels, from Marketing Assistant to Country Director. It was a strength that supercharged my career, helping my not-much-above-average product management skills shine and leading influencers around me to be confident that I could deliver results. Thanks to my presentations, I gained resources that helped me deliver more and gave me more success to present.

I observed closely what impact pitching skills had on my colleagues. Those who were poor at it were always underrated, while those who were strong at pitching were overrated. That created a gap of salary and title, but more importantly, the ability to pitch influenced levels of responsibility and the chance to work on cool projects, or not.

Most significantly, **people listen to those who can present well, and they listen less to those who can't.**

Being listened to is a fundamental human need. I saw how the ability to present affected people's sense of self-worth and their personal and professional sense of pride. Failing in front of an audience can break the presenter's confidence. Yet nailing a great pitch is a massive source of satisfaction and a huge confidence builder. *It simply feels great.*

In a large company, you can survive if you can't pitch. The lack of skill may influence whether you have a more satisfying career, and may mean you don't get the recognition you deserve for your work. Yet you can still earn a decent living, although the skill of presenting your work in a time-limited pitch is increasingly demanded among my corporate clients.

However, if you work in a startup, or anything to do with innovation, **you cannot survive if you cannot pitch.** There is not a single successful or well-funded startup in the world that does not have a great pitcher. The same goes for corporate innovation teams. They need a powerful evangelist to move stakeholders into action.

Startups and innovation teams pitch on average 25 times per day. We think consciously of pitches to investors and customers. Yet less obvious are the pitches to partners, mentors and potential employees, or at network events, or even at the coffee machine! In fact, each and every talk you have with anyone who might be able to help you get one step closer to realising your dream is a pitch.

Investors make decisions based on your pitch. I've spoken to many, and they believe your communication ability is critical to the value of your company.

"Pitching skills can add 5-20 percent to the exit value of a startup. The ability to communicate the quality of a product, team and business in a great pitch has a huge influence on a startup's success." — *Frank Appeldoorn, Arches Capital.*

Investors assess whether you can convince not only them, but also everyone else you will ever need to bring over the line in order to succeed.

No investor makes an investment decision based on a pitch alone, but without a pitch, nothing happens.

No management team or Board decides to invest cash and people into an innovation project based on a pitch, but every commitment decision started with a pitch.

Welcome to *Pitch to Win*. You've come to the right place to start changing your business future.

0.1.1 **Why is pitching so difficult?**

It's hardly a secret that pitching is important. So why are so many pitches so incredibly bad?

Talking too much, loose openings, poor closings, no clear structure, not finishing on time, detail-heavy slides, delivering in monotone, constant pacing, speaking too fast... we've all seen this happen. So why, when there is such massive value in getting it right, do so many pitchers get it so wrong?

I believe there are three major reasons.

First: No one is taught this skill at school. Students make presentations and are given feedback, but never provided any practical tools to make better pitches. When you have your first pitch, someone sends you the company template – bullet points galore – and you fill it in.

This book helps you catch up on that lost opportunity in your school years and gives you the tools to learn the art of pitching. It provides tried and tested, practical tools to help you get started on improving your pitches immediately.

Second: Most trainings and books about presentation focus on how you deliver: body language, vocals and presence. While these are extremely important, they are only one part of the process of delivering a great pitch. I've seen how critical it is to get convinced about your story. With conviction comes a reduction of stress, and delivery becomes more natural as a result.

You'll find tools in this book that will help you think creatively and build a strong and persuasive story line that you can stand solidly behind. You'll find out how to make great slides that add professionalism and impact to your pitch. You'll also find all the guidance you need about body language and voice to ensure you feel confident when it really matters. On top of all that, you'll find some powerful methods of managing nerves.

22

Third: This is human work. At the moment of truth – the first second when you start speaking – it simply comes down to one human being in front of other human beings giving his or her pitch.

Talking in front of an audience is one of the most vulnerable moments in a person's life. I've heard advice such as – "Just be yourself". However, almost no-one is equipped with the skills to deal with the pressure of public speaking without help or guidance.

The key is to have tools at hand to manage the experience of being under pressure in front of an audience, and to invest time in advance so that you are well prepared.

Having a clear understanding of the audience and an objective for the pitch, working on a carefully structured story with a well-crafted set of visuals, and having a practice and delivery approach that works will turn your nerves into positive energy.

By putting in the work and doing the exercises in this book, you'll put yourself in a great position to deliver a powerful and persuasive pitch.

0.1.2 **Who this book is for: Entrepreneurs and intrapreneurs**
This book is designed for startups and corporate innovation teams.

Pitching has generally been associated with startups until recent years. Large events such as WebSummit, The Next Web, TechCrunch and Slush regularly feature hundreds of startups on stage, telling their whole business stories in three to five minutes. Demo Days, Pitch Competitions, and even *Dragons' Den* have all contributed to an explosion of startup pitches since the turn of the millennium.

Now the pitch is growing beyond the startup world. Most major corporations are running innovation projects to transform their heavy business structures into leaner, more agile multi-disciplinary development teams. They apply Lean

Startup, the Business Model Canvas, Customer Development and Value Proposition techniques, which eventually all end up in a pitch.

What's the difference between startup and corporate innovation pitches?
Almost nothing! Both are time pressured, with a need for clarity on the problem, solution, uniqueness, business model and customer engagement. The biggest differences appear when pitching for resources, and pitching the team.

Usually, the number one resource a startup needs is money, followed by expertise and network. By working with numerous corporate innovation project teams, I've learned that, for them, the investment required is often more than money. Additional essentials include; time for the core team to develop their idea further; people from the organisation to commit time to working on the business; sponsorship at senior management and executive level; and possible inclusion of headcount and expenses in the mid-term plan.

When it comes to pitching the quality of the team, a startup tells why individuals in the core founding group and others brought into the team have the experience and drive to make it happen. In a corporate innovation project, the individuals who have brought the idea to this stage are less important. What matters more is which parts of the organisation need to be involved, which roles need to be created, and how the team should develop in size and skills.

These two major differences – team and investment – are highlighted as you walk through the steps to build your winning pitch. However, for the most part the tools needed to create a persuasive story are the same for these two types of pitchers.

Pitching to investors for money? Or to Board members for budget, time and resources? *Pitch to Win* will help you communicate the story you really want to tell and supercharge the chances of getting the result you want from your audience.

24

0.1.3 What kinds of pitches will this book prepare you for?

There are various phases of development you go through as a startup and corporate innovation team, and you'll need different kinds of pitches at each stage.

This book will prepare you especially for the early stages when pitching has the most impact, to share your idea, communicate the value of what you are doing and getting noticed. I call this the Glory Pitch, where there may be a series of teams at an event, a competition or a Demo Day. The goal is to catch attention and get the right people to engage with you afterwards.

By following the steps in this book, you'll also become prepared for the meetings that ideally follow the Glory Pitch, a one-hour follow-up meeting with an investor or the Board.

In that meeting, it will be much more interactive and less of a typical pitch. Getting prepared using the Pitch Canvas© and following the advice on how to prepare your slides will help you in these meetings too. Compared to the Glory Pitch, it will be less about body language and presentation skills, and more about content and having a solid, well-thought-out plan.

Whatever moment you're preparing for, this book will give you practical steps and tools to get your message across in the most persuasive way possible.

0.1.4 How I wrote this book: Learning by doing

Over the last years, I've spent thousands of hours coaching thousands of professionals and startups to pitch. The first thing I did – and never stopped doing – was to talk with people who hear pitches. I questioned them about what they want to hear and what annoys them; what catches their attention and imagination, what causes alarm bells to ring, and switches them off. This was the basis of my journey to help great ideas be heard.

I developed a pitch workshop by trying out all kinds of exercises with a wide variety of startups and corporate innovation teams in over 25 countries. Each time I ran the workshop, I looked for what helped my clients the most. My number one objective was not that people understand *how* to give a better pitch, but rather, that they can actually *do* it! I learned that the more I broke the workshop down into small, practical tasks that my clients could do in a few minutes, the faster they created a higher-quality pitch.

26

Feedback on what works and what doesn't has come to me in a variety of ways. Some who came to workshops would Tweet what they liked best, others would email me or send messages via LinkedIn. I got feedback from Accelerator organisers after their Demo Day, and through my workshop questionnaire. Most of all, I regularly saw the result of my work when my clients pitched on stage.

As a result, *Pitch to Win* contains only tools that work. Everything has been tried and tested, and turned into real action that you can take to elevate your pitches. That's why, throughout the book, you'll find numerous exercises that help you get closer to telling the story you really want to tell.

You can't think yourself into a great pitch
This is a DO book, not just a THINK book. You'll find practical exercises for everything, and each piece of theory and insight comes with a tool that you can use straight away in your next pitch. There is no long learning lead-time. This is a skill you can make quantum leaps in, within days. You just have to focus and do the work.

I realise you don't have time to waste, which is why the exercises usually take between 5 and 15 minutes. Push yourself to think fast and write content down: often the first thing you think of is the most powerful and most true to your real intention.

After doing the work, you'll have a clear roadmap and a process to follow which will shrink your preparation time, and empower the quality and effectiveness of every single pitch you ever do.

0.1.5 Pitch or presentation?

While working at Canon, I sat through over a million PowerPoint slides during long, impersonal, wide-ranging and information-heavy presentations without a clear objective.

In the last years, I've seen over five thousand pitches. The best were short and focused on the highlights only, with a clear ask and a personal edge.

It doesn't matter whether we call it a pitch or a presentation. We know which type of communication we want to hear when we're the audience, and we know which one we should deliver when pitching or presenting.

TED Talk or investor pitch, employee motivation or new product launch. Pitch it concisely with clarity, certainty and passion, and you'll have a massive chance of winning the audience over.

A presentation just sort of happens.
A pitch is an **Occasion**.

Pitching is the New Presentation.

0.1.6 Some people are born to do it... right?

There is a myth that some presenters can get on stage and inspire effortlessly, thanks to some magic in their character. Let me remove this myth here and now.

There are 0,1 percent of people on the earth with the ability to 'wing it'. For the rest of us: making great pitches is just work. It's about learning what works, following a process to implement proven tools into your own approach, and putting the hours in.

This book doesn't tell you exactly what to say: instead, it gives you the framework for you to find your story, and how to organise that story in a way that gets the results you want from your audience.

You too were born to pitch.

0.1.7 **Keep it real, read this book while preparing for an actual pitch**
The most useful approach to this book is to think of a pitch you have coming up in the next weeks or months. Simply trying to pick up a few tips is an option, but if you put all that's offered into action immediately for an actual pitch, you will instantly make a jump in the quality of your communication.

Focus on a real audience, a real objective, a real ask, and get some content written down and tested out with that pitching occasion in mind.

Here's the basis of a great pitch
I advise my clients to break things down into threes. (See chapter 1.3, on page 92 for why.) Here are my three big things about pitching.

28

Script.
Design.
Deliver.

Get the story straight in a great script.

Design visuals that support your story.

Deliver with certainty, commitment and passion.

Everything you need to know about pitching comes down to these three. I'll take you through each one, step by step.

Let's get to work!

We've gathered videos of the best pitches to help you with the concepts we describe in the book. You'll find QR codes at relevant points, where you can access the video examples instantly.

PRINS CONSTANTIJN VAN ORANJE-NASSAU

Startup envoy at Startup-Delta, the organisation for supporting startup development in the Netherlands.

Why does pitching matter?

Firstly, it forces the team to think about what they are really selling. Having to get the story out there before a critical audience is a good way to discipline yourself, to bring your message down to the essentials.

When I listen to a team pitching, I often realise that they don't fully understand exactly what their market is. They'll talk about the 10 to 20 things they are doing, rather than the single core element which is their true value proposition, and that becomes clear to the pitcher when they are under pressure to tell their story. That disciplining effect is really important.

Secondly, a pitch helps being ready to capitalise on an opportunity. There might be a potential client, an investor, or a potential employee that you want to impress at any moment. Having a story ready and being able to produce it in a convincing manner on the spot when it most counts, is a truly valuable asset.

What goes wrong with pitches?

Most of all, not understanding the audience. Your ability to adapt the message to the audience you're trying to convince is crucial. It's like a football match. Sometimes you have long passes, sometimes short passes. Your tactics need to respond to the circumstances.

You might have everything clear in a solid storyline, yet targeted to the wrong audience. For example, in a tech conference or a TEDx Talk, you need to inspire and share your personal story of how you came to your discoveries. However, in front of an investor group that inspiration part might be relevant but has to be much shorter. They will say: "Nice story,

29

but we've heard nice stories before. What will you deliver, when, what's the value proposition, where's the money coming from, which business are you going to replace or disrupt?"

Does a so-called Elevator Pitch matter? Pitching when you've got those 30 seconds with an influential person?
That's about timing! I get pitched at a lot, and often at the wrong moments. For example, at a reception or a launch party, someone's shouting in your ear and you're half deaf from them yelling their business plan at you. They hit the start button and never stop... I wonder to myself, why would they think I might be interested in their business at that particular moment? If it's a party, where you exchange more on a personal level, this might not be the moment when I or others are most receptive. Pitching at the wrong time is also a big mistake people make.

We learn from the idea of the Elevator Pitch that we must be able to deliver at any moment. But you might want to think about whether you SHOULD deliver at that moment! As you share your pitch, try to sense your audience's mood and be a little dynamic about how much you tell. Naturally you need to deliver your message, but also understand that when someone's twitching in their chair, they are bothered by something. Rather than speeding up, you can stop and ask a question, engage them in a different way. That sensitivity to the audience is often missed.

What's more important, passion or content?
It starts with passion and then it's about content. If someone doesn't have the passion and you don't get engaged as a listener, then you wonder: "How is this person going to deliver?" Then again, it's also about execution. I need to gain some confidence in their ability to convert that passion into real action and business. Passion is what you capture the attention with and once my attention is captured, I want to know the How.

For you, what impact does a great pitch have?

A great pitch makes the listener want to make a deal immediately! It gives them the feeling that if they don't act now, the opportunity will walk out of the door. A great pitch should have a combination of vision that really captures the imagination, and proof of execution on the journey towards making that vision reality. That combination makes the audience want to grab the moment and take action now.

They've got 30 seconds to pitch to you, what do you want to hear?

I want truly to understand what the value proposition is and what the person expects from me. Give me an action, a next step.

Do you have any last advice?

Take cultural differences into consideration and adjust delivery according to the people you are presenting to. And get training. Not just on preparing the storyline, but also on these cultural aspects of different nationalities and sensitivities.

It doesn't start and stop with the pitch, you need to follow up and keep going through all the steps to make a deal. Asking questions is a very underrated part of pitching too, because sometimes you learn more and get more response from your audience by asking them to get involved. ●

31

SCRIPT.

ONE

1.1.1 Stop! Don't open PowerPoint!

The first step is to get the story straight, and decide what content, in which order, you will tell.

My strongest advice at this moment is:

Don't open PowerPoint!

Or Keynote, or Prezi, or whatever you use to create slides. Work on the storyline first.

Most people think: "I've got a pitch coming up on Thursday. Better get the slides done!" They open the laptop and immediately try to translate their thoughts into some kind of logical order, while working in slide software. *This is an impossible task.*

As soon as you start to work on slides, you get caught up in the technical work of slide design. While thinking what your story is, you write something down and begin to wonder:

- "Should this text be 32 points or 36 points?"
- "Should it be left or right aligned?"
- "Should the text be **bold** or normal?"
- "Which picture goes with this idea to make it clearer?"
- "Should the background be blue or green?"

And so on.

This questioning means your attention flips between the message you want to bring and how the slide will emphasise that story. Doing these two things simultaneously makes you extremely inefficient and increases your preparation time by many hours.

On top of this, you never see the whole presentation. You keep switching backwards and forwards through the slide

35

deck, trying to see if it is logical and if it flows. Meanwhile, the whole presentation is in your head and focused on a very internal process. You've been working to make slides instead of identifying the story that will resonate with the audience.

I did exactly the same during my 16 years at Canon, and never understood why I felt so frustrated making slide presentations. In the last few years, I've created a new approach to building a pitch, which I share with all my clients and is now working for thousands of people.

That approach begins with thinking about some big factors that influence the success – or otherwise – of your pitch. And it involves a revolutionary tool that will save you 20 to 30 percent of preparation time for every pitch you ever make. *I'm going to give you days of your life back!*

It starts with the audience. Before touching any presentation software, you need to tune your thoughts and actions towards three things. Who is the audience?

What is the objective of the pitch? And which parts of my story do I need to tell to influence the audience and reach that objective?

Once you have this in place, you can start to structure how to tell that story in the most effective way. But first, let's get clear on who we are talking to and what we are trying to achieve.

1.1.2 Communication is what the listener does

Lance Miller told me this phrase from management guru Peter Drucker back in 1992, and it has been a powerful guide for every pitch I've given and every pitcher I've trained ever since.

You don't want simply to *tell* your story. Instead, you want the listener to *do* something.

The starting point is: Who is the listener? What type of people will hear the pitch? What drives her? What keeps him awake at night? What do they care about?

36

Taking time to understand your audience will make your objective so much easier to achieve. Here are a few examples of potential audiences you might pitch to and what kind of content they may be interested in.

When you're pitching your next big project to the Board, they'll want to know about results and money.

Face to face with impact investors? They want to understand how your positive effect on society or environment will be sustainable with a solid business plan.

Do you need to convince sales and marketing people to get behind your product? They're probably not going to be hooked by the process you've followed to develop your idea; instead, focus on results, what they can do with these results, and how you help them achieve their targets.

Engineers? Show them what's under the hood and share some tech innovation to excite them.

VCs (venture capitalists) are interested in big opportunities to scale your business into a huge market. Show ambition and the size of the opportunity.

If you make the exact same pitch of your concept to all of the above audiences, it simply won't succeed because you're not tuned in to all their various interests. You're only pushing your own message.

This is not about: "Telling them what they want to hear." It's about looking at all the many elements of your proposition and selecting those points that will resonate with your audience based on *their* interests. Doing so will increase the chance they will take the action you need.

ACTION

Action – 5-minute task – Write down who your audience is and what they care about?

Spend five minutes writing down a short profile of your audience. The following questions will help you get started, but don't limit your profile of the audience to these points. Write down everything you can think of.

1. What do they care about?
2. What are their biggest challenges?
3. Are they conservative or innovative? *(Note: sometimes people say they're innovative when in fact they are actually conservative, but just want to have things a little better! And some people really want to change the world and turn* an industry on its head. Which one is your audience?)
4. Are they technical and want to know how things work?
5. Are they money focused? If so, are they interested in reducing cost, increasing turnover, more profit, 10x growth, or gradual improvement?
6. Are they interested in social impact? The environment?
7. Do they care about details, or do they tend to be interested in headlines only?
8. Are they theoretical or doers? Do they want to know the thinking behind the idea, or just the outcomes?

38

When you make your pitch script, come back to these descriptions of your audience and the questions they may be asking themselves, and ensure you've covered what they are expecting.

What if there is a mixed audience?
In this case, it's about identifying whom you need to influence. For example, if you have an audience of fifty people but only three decision makers, it's best to focus

on these three people for this exercise and target your message to them first. It could be that you miss the mark with the remainder of the audience, but if you persuade the decision makers, then you've reached your goal.

1.1.3 You want them to do...what? Be clear on the objective

It might seem obvious that you should have a clear goal for your pitch in terms of action you want the audience to take. However, most pitchers are too focused on telling their stories, or they focus only on the bigger, long-term goals, winning the investment or getting the sales.

I often ask my clients, "What do you want the audience to do as a result of your pitch?" They reply with statements like: "I want them to understand what we are trying to do," or "We need them to support the project," or "I want them to believe in our product." For any of these outcomes to happen, you need to define and clearly state your Call To Action.

Therefore, to make the most of your pitch, it's essential to identify two objectives.

Firstly, what's the big goal? For example: Gain €500K investment. Get approval of a €1 million budget and a five-person full-time team for the project to go ahead. Believe in the product. Solve world poverty.

Secondly, what's the first next step the audience can take on the journey towards your big goal? This step needs to be something they can do, not just think.

For the big goals given as examples above, the actions would look like this:

Big goal	Immediate first-next step objective
$500K investment	Get a one-hour meeting arranged with the investor
Approval of budget/team	Inspire them to read a proposal, in preparation for a go/no-go meeting
Belief in our product	Trigger them to download the free version at the App Store and try it out
Solve world poverty	Get them to visit your website and donate something

Think of the objective as: The morning after the pitch, what can they do? What can they click, who can they call, what will they read, who will they introduce you to? Most importantly, they click to accept your invitation for a follow-up meeting.

40

ACTION

Action – 2-minute task – What's the objective?
Write down the following:
1. What's the big objective of this pitch? Write it down.
2. What's the first next step you want the audience to take to get them closer to your big objective? Write it down.

Get your story straight and get it out of your head
Now that you're clear on who the audience is and what the pitch objective is, the next step is to get some useful content written down. You might be tempted to reach for the computer and start creating slides.

Once again, stop!

There is plenty more thinking and writing down to be done before you even create the title slide. First, you need to get the story straight.

The simplest and fastest path to establishing your story is to brainstorm using Post-it® notes.

Brainstorm
with Post-its®

You've probably been involved in Post-it® brainstorms before – over 90 percent of professionals have. Yet less than 10 percent of the thousands of people I've coached had used the same methods to prepare their pitches before coming to my workshops.

Building your story with Post-it® notes will help you think creatively and organise your thoughts in a logical order. You'll be able to see the whole story from top to bottom and get a feel for where you are strong, and what needs to be made more concrete. I have created a tool called the Pitch Canvas© to help you do so in a structured way.

1.2 SCRIPTING WITH THE PITCH CANVAS®

1.2.1 How to brainstorm your pitch using Post-its®

Here is a quick overview of the process to follow. We'll revisit this process in more detail after I've explained the Pitch Canvas© to take you through it step-by-step.

To begin with, take plenty of Post-it® notes, some marker pens and a flipchart. (A few sheets of paper stuck together to form a bigger sheet will also work if you don't have a flipchart.) Then open your mind and write some thoughts down, ideally with some members of your team. It can also be done as an individual.

The same rules apply as in any brainstorm:
- Write down everything you can think of that you might say in the pitch. Keep it to keywords and short phrases, not full sentences.
- Write down one idea per Post-it®, not five sentences on one sticky! You need to be flexible with moving the ideas around so you can reorder and select later.
- Keep writing until you run out of ideas. All ideas are *possibilities* in the initial stage, so don't focus on which are good or bad until everything is written down.
- Once all ideas are down, go through a selection process. Review your audience and objective, and consider

41

the length of the pitch. These steps will guide you on which parts of your brainstorm to focus your storyline on. Put all Post-its® that don't fit this selection aside until you are complete and feel confident they are no longer needed.

- Remove duplication, put aside any non-relevant points, and start to cluster the Post-its® around big issues that really matter.
- Finally, based on the remaining Post-its®, create a set of chapter headings using different-coloured Post-its®. What is the backbone of the pitch? What will you tell per chapter? Organise the content Post-its® around the chapter headings.

These three steps – rough brainstorm, cluster and select, and organise into chapter headings – will help you clarify the story you want to tell, and give a complete view of the pitch.

This is the process, but doing so in one jump can be hard. What if you have no idea what the investors, jury or innovation Board members are looking for? What exactly should you brainstorm in the first place, to focus on the right elements of your business in your pitch – the ones your audience wants to hear and that make the biggest persuasive impact?

This is where the Pitch Canvas© comes in.

The Pitch Canvas©

An entrepreneurial brainstorming tool that helps you structure and visualise your pitch on one page .

Simple Statement of what change you and your product are making in the world.
A memorable one-sentence explanation of what you do for customers.

Pain (+ Gain)
What problem are you solving for your customers?
What does the pain result in?
Can you make the pain a human problem, that everyone can relate to?
How many people need this problem solved - market size?
Have you validated that people will pay to have it solved?

Product
As simply as possible: what does your product do for customers?
What opportunities do you provide for people to be faster, more cost-effective, more efficient, happier, safer?
How does it work?
How have you tested it with customers?
(Be sure not to let the product dominate the pitch.)

Product Demo
Live demo? (always risky, but powerful if it works...)
A screenflow movie of a working app convinces this is for real. Physical product convinces you can execute.
Screenshots are also OK, but can look like a mock-up - moving product on screen is better.
Can you show a real customer using it?

What's Unique
Technology/Relationships/Partnerships.
How do you help your customers get results differently to your competition, or alternatives?
Show you have researched the market and know what competition is out there.

Customer Traction
Success so far?
Pilot customers? Major brands?
Progression in users or downloads?
Customer reference quotes or movies?
PR coverage? Competition wins?
Use data and facts to strengthen your case.

Business Model
How do you get paid?
What's the opportunity for growth?
How can you scale beyond your current scope: new industries, territories, applications of partnerships and technology?

Investment
Have you invested money yourself?
Have you raised money so far?
How much are you looking for now?
What big next steps will you use the investment for?
What milestones will you reach with the money?
How many, and what type of investor are you looking for?
What expectations do you have of your investors; network, expertise?

Team
What relevant experience and skills does your team have that supports your story?
Brands worked for? Achievements? Sales success?
What binds you together as people and as entrepreneurs to fix this problem?
What's special about the character of your team, that will make you stand out and be memorable?

Call To Action and End Statement
Finish the pitch strongly with a clear request for the audience to take action - what is their first next step?

Why You?
NOTE: Why You? can show up in any part of the pitch.
Why do you care about solving this problem for your customers? How has your life been affected by this industry and business?
Why should your audience have confidence that you are driven to do what you promise, no matter what?

 Best 3 Minutes

Please feel free to share The Pitch Canvas©.
Ensure you reference Best3Minutes.com after each use.

1.2.2 **Your brainstorming tool:**
The Pitch Canvas© explained
In 2013, I started working with my first 40 startups. We did many brainstorm sessions together, which were pretty random and time consuming. I began to realise that there had to be a more efficient way to structure the process of brainstorming, and began to realise there was a pattern to the content required for a successful pitch.

I created the Pitch Canvas© to help start-ups and innovation teams know what to talk about and what not to talk about, so that investors and Board members would sit up and take notice. It's a one-page storytelling tool that enables you to visualise and structure your pitch on one page.

The Pitch Canvas© has been tested by over 700 startups that I worked with directly, and has been downloaded tens of thousands of times. It's also been used by organisations such as ING, Philips, Booking.com, Unilever, IKEA and TEDx as a tool to guide pitches of all kinds.

I developed it by talking with numerous investors, innovation Board members and pitch competition jury members to understand what they expect to see and hear. I sat in on investor sneak previews, Demo Days, hackathons and VC interviews, spending time to talk with everyone about what made an impact in any pitch.

The Pitch Canvas© has gone through over forty revisions, because all this research has given me fuel to keep improving and shaping the content, questions and design. You can find the most up-to-date version at Best3minutes.com.

One thing to note: the Pitch Canvas© is structured in a way to make it easy to brainstorm, but you *don't* have to pitch in the order of the Pitch Canvas© (although if you have no idea where to start, it's not a bad way to build your pitch). Feel free to mix it up and create your own unique approach.

You also don't have to include every item in every pitch. The eleven blocks of

44

potential content help you think through all the elements you might want to talk about. Depending on the audience, your objective and how many minutes you have to pitch, you'll select the points you need to talk about. Another advantage of brainstorming on all elements of the Pitch Canvas© is that you'll find you are prepared for Q&A sessions, where more details are required.

Now let's see what the Pitch Canvas© is made up of, find out what kinds of topics your audience may want to hear in your pitch and brainstorm some content to set you on your way to building your best storyline.

Simple Statement

The Simple Statement expresses the change you and your product are making in the world; a memorable one-sentence explanation of what you do for customers.

Those who see your pitch will never make decisions on the spot. You need people to talk about you with others – to be able to pass on in one sentence what you do and the value you bring.

It's not a description of your product: for example, it's not saying, "We have an app that has a lot of 3D printing templates." Rather, it might be, "We're making 3D printing easy and accessible for the world." Your Simple Statement should be one level up from the product and closer to the vision of your proposition.

Here's another example from a well-known company. If you were pitching WeTransfer, you wouldn't say, "We have a website where you can send large files to people." But that would be a simple (and pretty boring) product description.

Instead WeTransfer states: "Our mission is to enable the effortless transfer of ideas, from one creative mind to many." This way they could solve the problem in various ways – with a website, a cloud

45

service, an app, or even couriers traveling the earth carrying hard drives! But what they make clear is who they are targeting (people who create), the number one value (effortless) and that it's all about ideas being shared (ideas from one to many). It shows ambition, instead of just what they do.

As you form your own Simple Statement, bear in mind that your product will constantly change. However, the problem you are fixing, the industry you are addressing and the value you're bringing to customers are likely to remain constant. Keep it on a semi-high level; you can be more specific about your product later in the pitch.

How do you develop a Simple Statement? Although this is something you might tell near the beginning of the pitch, it's a statement you will probably develop at the end of your brainstorm.

At this point you've thought everything through, you'll have clarity on many

points of value and it will be easier to create this statement. Nevertheless, try the following exercise and see how far it brings you. It's always possible to come back to this exercise.

Note: Here are a few cliché phrases to avoid!

- "Changing the way we..."
- "Making the world a better place by..."
- "Disrupting the XYZ industry..."

Action – 10-minute task – Brainstorm your Simple Statement.

Write on separate Post-its®:

1. All key words about the value you bring.
2. Who you bring value for.
3. The industry that you are in.
4. Your highest mission.

Try forming a single sentence out of these words to capture the change you are bringing into the world.

ACTION

46

If you're struggling with this, come back to it after going through the other blocks of the Pitch Canvas©.

A quick reminder: make sure to save the Post-its® from all the exercises because you will need them later on. You can use the 3M Post-it® Plus app (iOS only, unfortunately) for capturing your brainstorms, and you can export them as a pdf.

Pain (and Gain)

All investors and Board members tell me the same thing: "I need to understand clearly what problem is being fixed."

They even say, "If there is no problem fixed, the product has no purpose." Being crystal clear on the pain is an essential part of any pitch, and is the issue you should spend the most time on.

There are three major questions that investors and Board members are asking:
- Is there a real problem, that causes genuine frustration, inefficiency and complexity? Is it an irritation or a true pain?
- Is that problem big: Are there huge numbers of people who need this problem fixed?
- Have you validated that people will pay to have this problem fixed?

You need to demonstrate that there's a serious pain that large volumes of people are desperate to solve: it's the backbone of your proposition.

It's not only about describing what the pain is – it's especially about what it results in. Can you make the pain human and something that everyone can relate to?

Humans respond to problems. Intrinsically we are programmed by deep instinct to look for solutions to problems, and when things are going well, we pay little attention.

47

As an example: walk into your working space on Monday morning and say, "I had a really nice weekend," and those around you will respond casually with a polite, "That's nice...," and that will be the end of it.

However, if you announce, "You won't believe it – I got fined by the police for something really stupid on Friday." Response: "Really? What happened? What did you do? How much did you get fined?" And you've got their attention.

You might want to tell in your pitch, "We're giving joy with our product!" But there is always a pain that needs to be solved. Ask yourself what people are triggered by to pay attention and jump into action.

Do they say, "I wish I could spend more time with my children." Or do they shout, "I wish I could stop wasting time!" The trigger is the negative – the Pain. The benefit is the positive – the Gain.

"It comes down to bad outcomes, risks and obstacles to getting things done."
— Alexander Osterwalder, *Value Proposition Design*.

Pitching the pain you are fixing has a lot to do with connecting the problem with the audience. It's not just about describing the problem, but rather what the problem results in for real people – and that turns it into a pain that the audience can associate with.

For example, a team I coached called Mobypark didn't pitch their product by saying, "Parking is difficult. We've got an app for that." Anyone that doesn't have a car, or doesn't find parking difficult will respond, "Who cares? If you can't park, take the bus!"

Instead, Mobypark pitched the human result of the parking problem.

"Can you imagine we spend over 20 minutes on average every time we look for a parking space? That means while

48

drivers are going round in circles, looking for that elusive space, their families are sitting down to dinner, without them, again. Or their best friends are gathered in the bar, anticipating the kick off of the game they've been waiting for all season, about to have their first drink. Meanwhile the driver is still in the car, hunting, and it drives them nuts!"

Even if you don't have a car, you are very likely to associate with the pain of missing out on these kinds of experiences. Audiences collectively nodded their head as Mobypark pushed home a quantified description of the pain they were addressing

There are several ways to describe the Pain:

- Tell a personal story: you explain your own connection to, or experience of, the problem you are fixing. It could also be about friends, family or close work colleagues.
- Give facts: user data that show the size of the problem, and market data that show the size of the opportunity.
- Describe individual cases: make it personal, about one specific person who experiences the problem, and then connect that person to the larger market.

Focus on condensing the pain into a concise and clear description of the problem in a way that your audience can identify with.

As Patrick de Zeeuw, co-founder of Startupbootcamp, says, "Stick in the fork, then twist it – and twist it again. Make sure they can feel the pain!"

Describing the pain is also a moment to explain the market size. Doing so is tricky, because telling the macro market size (for example, "The parking market is worth 50 billion Euros globally") feels very general. However, painting a picture of a large opportunity and how you plan to take a piece of it can be powerful.

I would recommend describing the larger market and then define the specific part you are addressing. For example:

"There are 400,000 accountants in country X, 10 million across the whole of Europe and 25 million worldwide. We are targeting the 11 percent of that group who use software Y and struggle with problem Z."

ACTION

Action – 15-minute task – Brainstorm your Pain and Gain.
Write on Post-its®:
1. What is the problem you're solving? Who has that problem?
2. What's the human result of the pain? How is it affecting real people's lives?
3. How big is that problem? How many people have the pain – in your country, in your continent, in the world? Is the opportunity big?
4. What validation is there that people will pay to have it solved?

Note: This might take more than the 15 minutes recommended! Have a first try at it, and debate it among your team. It's the hardest piece of the pitch to finalise, and worth investing time to get it right. If needed, see the Value Proposition Canvas by Alexander Osterwalder for more ideas on Pain and Gain. Once you've established the pain clearly, you'll find it much easier to build the rest of the pitch.

Product

Describing the product is the part that most of us excel in. But there are some essential points to bear in mind.

You are not pitching your product. You are pitching the business created by your ability to develop and execute solutions to the huge problem you have identified, as well as the size of the opportunity.

Product
explained

A product without a problem or a business model, or without enough customers who will pay to have it fixed is not a business, it's a hobby. A product without a team who can execute, learn, engage with customers and take it to the next level is doomed to failure, and of no interest to investors or Board members.

Especially in an investor or innovation Board pitch, these stakeholders are not expecting you to have the perfect product. They are looking to see whether you can execute and create solutions based on customer interaction and validation.

Therefore, while explaining your product is naturally important, the key is not to get lost in the details. Explain in simple terms what it does and how it benefits customers.

The technology behind the product is not the most important thing either so keep the description away from deep tech. However, if you have a part of the technology IP protected, do mention this.

Your product does not have to be complete at the moment you are pitching. Tell your audience how it performs now, and if you have some great stuff in development that you are very confident will be delivered in the coming months, tell about those aspects of your product too. Share a vision of what the product could deliver for customers.

In short, focus less on what your product does and more on what your customers can do with your product.

Coming back to the parking app example, you could say: "Our app analyses all the parking spaces in the immediate vicinity, using a blend of artificial intelligence and Internet of Things sensors to pinpoint precise geo positions of available parking spaces." (And watch the audience's eyes glaze over as you do!)

However, it's more effective to tell about the value for the user. "Drivers get to find a parking space faster, and cheaper, with no hassle, thanks to one simple 'Find me

51

a space NOW!' button. They're parked within three minutes."

Talking about a product has a limited value, and your task is to select the absolute essential items to tell. One of the most effective ways to explain the product is to show it, so if there's time, get them into a demo as fast as you can.

52

Action – 10-minute task – Brainstorm your product.
Write on Post-its®:
1. As simply as possible, what does your product do for customers?
2. What opportunities do you provide for people to be faster, more cost-effective, more efficient, happier, safer?
3. How does it work?
4. Who is the product targeted at?

Product Demo

As one investor said to me when I asked him what he really wanted from a pitch: "Get me onto the product as quickly as possible, and let me see what you've built. Then I can find out whether you are a dreamer or a person who executes her dreams."

Demonstrating a working product proves that you have done more than simply think about the issues you are addressing. You've actually built something of value to customers.

The question is, how are you going to demonstrate your product?

Physical examples
It would be great to have some real prototypes or production samples to show. I've seen a terrific chocolate company, Ridiculously Good, dish out products to the

Product Demo
explained

jury at a pitch competition, providing an instant 'taste' of the proposition!

Handing the product round is effective, but if not managed well, can be distracting. With larger audiences, I advise to show a picture of the product on screen as well as having it in your hand, as they may not be able to see it otherwise.

Software

There are three main options to demonstrate software products.

The first option is to make a short animation movie of the features, using tools such as Powtoon, Videoscribe or Moovly. This has the advantage of speed – you can tell a lot in a conceptual way and cover a lot of ground in a very short time and in a style that's not too serious. The downside is that an animation doesn't prove you have a working product. In fact, it even strongly suggests you are in the idea stage only.

Secondly, you could show some screen shots of the product to highlight some of the best stuff inside. However, static shots still feel like a mock-up and not necessarily a working product.

The third option is the one I find most effective – an animated screenflow of the app working. This way, the audience gets more of a sense of a real product that people can actually buy and you can get feedback on.

A screenflow movie is the option most likely to convince you have a business, not just an idea. Keep it short – 20 to 30 seconds would be optimal, but if the pitch is very short (three minutes or less) then even a 15-second clip can still communicate, "We have a working product."

Ensure that whatever you show about the product is valuable and not just process. Logins, lines of customer data and transactions, and long transitions from one step to another are not interesting at all. Edit the movie to focus only on a few aspects of the product that really stand out.

53

There is one more way to demo your software product, and that is LIVE. There are two reasons why I would strongly recommend you not to do it!

Firstly, as a pitcher you will need to focus on what to click at each moment, while concentrating on how to explain it. I've seen this go wrong so many times, simply because it takes your focus away from the audience.

Secondly, there is a chance that it will not work! No matter how much you test, the pressure of a big pitch causes things to go wrong when you least expect it. Even if it's not your fault – say, the internet connection is down, or the Bluetooth on your iPhone is faulty – all the audience will remember is, *it didn't work!*

Stick to these recommended options if you can, showing the product physically, or making an on-screen animation of the app in action. This presentation of your product will build credibility and belief in you as a team and in your idea as a business.

Action – 10-minute task – Brainstorm your Product Demo.

Write on Post-its®:
1. What are the various ways you could demo your product?
2. Which features or aspects of your product do you want to focus on?
3. Is there one killer functionality you must show?

What's Unique

Board members and investors have told me that What's Unique is a very important part of the pitch. Showing What's Unique is about clarifying where your proposition falls in relation to customer needs, and in comparison with whatever else is out there serving those customer needs right now.

54

What's Unique
explained

Firstly, look at what is unique in terms of technology. It's rare that technology is truly unique. It's usually about how you apply that technology, and not the technology itself.

If there *is* something special about the tech, then tell them. Especially if you have a patent in progress or already established, or other protection of your IP, it's good to mention this. Having this kind of IP asset can add value to your company.

Secondly, look further than the technology. Maybe you have a unique partnership in product development together with a leading player in the industry. Or perhaps there is a unique way of bringing customers into the platform.

And thirdly, reflect on the competition. This can be a tricky one and depends on where you are pitching.

In Europe, it's not welcomed if you directly compare yourself with a competitor.

For example, you wouldn't say "We have a platform that runs three times faster than the leader in the industry, company X." However, in the US, comparative advertising is the norm, and you may need to go head to head with leading competitors.

One of the downsides of comparing to a specific company is that you give audience mindshare to that competitor. My recommended way of benchmarking with competition is to block several of them together.

For example, you could say: "There are various solutions on the market, such as A, B and C. What they offer is this..." Then you list up two or three of the features of those companies.

55

Next, describe that you offer all of this, and more. If there is one killer feature that truly stands out as making a difference to customers, make sure that gets the most focus.

Mentioning competition shows that you know the market. It can also validate that there is a market for a solution to the problem you're addressing.

I've heard startups say: "There is no competition." Investors get really grumpy when they hear this! There is always some kind of alternative solution available, even if it's not designed for the task, or if it's a poor execution. Make sure they know that you know your playing field.

The final aspect of What's Unique is what I call the Hanging Question.

The Hanging Question is all about that one issue, or that one competitor, that keeps being mentioned, again and again, so that you get sick of it! Let me give you an example from a startup called 24Sessions.

When I met the team, they explained they had a video chat system. Within minutes, I questioned "Does anyone ask if you are like Skype?" They answered, with a roll of the eyes, "Absolutely, all the time!"

24Sessions offers a solution for companies such as banks to connect with their customers online. The customer can select an advisor, book an appointment, and leave a rating. Plus, the meetings are recorded, which is essential from a regulatory point of view.

The problem: if they don't directly mention Skype and explain why they have so much more to offer to a bank, then the audience could be distracted. It's as if a huge question mark is hanging right in front of their faces, and they can't think of anything except the question: "Isn't this just like Skype?"

Here's how 24Sessions dealt with their Hanging Question.

"So what sets us apart from Skype or other existing webcam advice initiatives? After all, we both do video chat. Well, for us, video chat is just a small piece of

56

the puzzle. We provide the total solution: search, schedule, video chat and review system in one service. Furthermore, 24Sessions is securely encrypted, works on every browser, is super simple to use, and you can style it in your own corporate identity."

With this explanation, they blow away any Hanging Questions about Skype, and position themselves way ahead of a recognised market leader.

Do you keep getting asked a specific question about your product, again and again? Put the issue on the table early on in the pitch and answer it. Otherwise that Hanging Question clouds your listeners' judgment, preventing them from focusing on the whole story.

Action – 10-minute task – Brainstorm What's Unique.

Write on Post-its®:

1. What sets your product aside from current or alternative solutions?
2. Do you have any unique technology? Is the IP protected?
3. Have you got any unique partnerships or co-development agreements?
4. Is there a Hanging Question which you need to answer in the pitch?

57

Customer traction

Everyone starts listening to a pitch assuming it's a concept, not a business. There are two ways to overcome that.

The first is showing a working product, which we already covered. The second is to show customer traction.

Customer traction is about social proof that people or companies believe in your business so much, that they have already paid for and used your product. It's also about showing that you can engage with customers and convince them. All this builds trust and credibility among your audiences.

If you already have sales and users, you have various options of showing progress.

You could talk about paid pilot customers – recognisable brands or organisations who have already bought into your product. Stating major brands that you are working with, or have pilot programs with, builds your credibility.

If you have a lot of traction, ensure that you focus on brands and organisations that are instantly familiar to the audience. For example, the 55-store test of your product in that huge supermarket, instantly recognisable to your home audience, may not mean anything in the US, because the supermarket brand

is unknown there. Ensure the audience understands the significance of the deal by explaining the position the customer holds in your own market.

You can also share features of your product in the words of your customers, and how they gain benefit from it. "The reason company X started working with us is because they love being able to..." This is way more powerful than stating the feature yourself.

Note: Be careful with testimonials in text and in movies. The danger is that they seem staged and false; make sure the language is in real spoken terms and not in written, more formal language. You can make this happen by interviewing the customers with carefully crafted questions that get them to emphasise the points you want to focus on, yet using their own words.

Nobody would really say, "Product X provides us an Open API that empowers us to access the underlying data to facilitate a

broader and deeper engagement with the essential customer base."

But they might say: "We love it: the open APIs give us the tools we need to engage with our customers, with less cost for us."

If you are a B2C company, it may be more about users. How many people have downloaded the app, or have paid for it? How many daily users do you have, and are there any simple user engagement metrics you can share?

Most important is to show development, rather than hard numbers. For example, if you have 2000 users, the audience instantly have an opinion. Is 2000 a lot, or is it too few? They may get it wrong and misunderstand the value of the number.

However, if you tell that your user base has grown by an average of 10 percent per month for the last six months, or you've doubled your daily users over the last quarter, there is no opinion needed. It's

clear progress and shows solid signs of uptake.

Don't be afraid to talk about revenue figures and growth. The hardest thing of all is to generate actual sales, and if you are doing so, then be ready to share that success.

You can mention one quick aspect of traction right at the beginning of your pitch, if there is an impressive figure or client, and expand later. The cliché on this goes: "Hi, this is who we are, this is what we do, and I am here to tell you why 10,000 users are already paying a monthly subscription for our service."

The value of this is that you give a clear message early in the pitch that people are already buying, and the audience should take you seriously. It tells that this is a business, not an idea. You then go on to talk about the pain, the product and other aspects of your proposition, and expand in a bit more detail about traction later in the pitch.

See if you can make a variation on this cliché. Try to tell it in a different way compared to other startups, so that you stand out among the crowd.

I'm often asked: "What if you are an early stage startup or innovation team, with no sales yet?" In that case, you can focus more on validation.

What have you done to test your ideas with real users? What customer interviews have you done? What have you learned, and how did you pivot?

It's all about proving that your concept has demand, which builds credibility that you are on the right track.

60

ACTION

Action – 15-minute task – Brainstorm your traction.
Write on Post-its®:
1. Do you have customers already? Who are they and are there any significant, recognisable brands?
2. Is there growth in users and/or revenue?
3. What usage data do you have? How about customer retention, or usage frequency data?
4. If you have no sales yet, what have you done to validate the proposition? Customer interviews? Online experiments? How have you engaged with potential customers?
5. Do you have an announcement? Is there a recent success that you can share as a new milestone of development?

Business model
explained

Business model

Establishing your business model is an ongoing process, and one that never stops. Many startups and innovation teams agonise over what to tell about their business model in their pitches, because at the exact moment they meet their audience, they haven't made a firm decision about which direction they are going.

Here's the truth: 90 percent of startups and innovation teams pitching for resources have no certain business model when they pitch – and that is no major problem.

What matters is to demonstrate that you know where the money is coming from potentially and how to construct a business model. If you're an advanced startup, you may need to show you've concluded the hunt for an effective business model; an early startup will need to make clear they know at least one way to monetise its solution to the problem.

The worst case is to tell that you are exploring various business models and then explain them all. Doing so gives a high chance of triggering someone to say, "You have no focus."

If you're not sure which business model to explain, show the one that you believe will be most lucrative at the moment you pitch, and hint at the fact that you are exploring others. This approach will show you are focusing, yet thinking ahead.

I once attended an investor sneak preview where ten startups pitched their businesses. A number of teams didn't explain their business model – and the investors I spoke to afterwards felt it was a critical error. Even if you are not certain of the absolute best monetisation model for your proposition, showing you have thought about where the money is coming from is essential.

61

I would recommend not mentioning actual pricing of your product or service. As soon as you say, "It costs €49 per month," you give the audience an opportunity to have an opinion. Almost guaranteed, some will think it's too high, and the rest will think it's too low! Focus on the mechanism of generating revenue, not the absolute amounts. In this case, I would advise to say: "We charge a monthly subscription fee."

You can explain in more detail during follow up meetings. If they ask, "How much does it cost?", you can share how you came to the price of €49, and what testing you have done to establish that this is the right price. Then you can put some context around the figure, and have a conversation about it. That's not possible in a pitch, because it would take too long.

In the pitch, you can also take the opportunity to talk a little about scaling. It might be that you can state: "We will establish ourselves in this country/market, and next year we will move to further countries/expand to other areas of the industry."

Once again, keep the focus – give a hint of the future, but make sure they understand what you are doing first to conquer your current markets and territories.

Finally, remember this is rational information. It's not easy to be passionate when explaining, "We take an eight percent commission from every transaction." Not very! Therefore, keep the business model explanation short, informational and to the point. Get on to the other good stuff as quickly as possible!

Action – 5-minute task – Brainstorm your business model.

Write on Post-its®:

1. As simply as possible, what's the business model?
2. If you are exploring various business models, write them all down. Then decide among you which one you will pitch.
3. Do you already have a scaling plan? New countries, new parts of your current industry, totally new industries?

Investment. Or: what do you need to make it happen?

This is one area where a startup and corporate innovation pitch can be very different. If you are an innovation team pitching to the Board, please jump to page 66.

For any startup, the decision to bring in investment should not be taken lightly. An investor is a new business partner who will give a cash injection, at a price.

That price involves: equity being given up; some autonomy being lost side by side with additional reporting responsibilities; and an increase in pressure, both perceived and real.

Nevertheless, most successful startups have required funding at some stage, and few have turned to profit without it. Getting investment can be the moment when your business turns from an idea to a scalable proposition. An investor can also bring in specific knowledge of an industry and network connections that can help your business grow.

Like the business model explanation, the key for pitching about the investment you need and what you plan to do with it is to inform the necessary rational content as efficiently as possible. Here's how.

63

Have you invested money yourself?
The answer indicates how much risk you have personally taken, and to some extent how much you believe in the concept yourself. This investment is about cash, not time. Most investors want you to live in a cardboard box for the first 10 years of the business until they see a 10x return! So while you can mention "I've invested €50K and two years of my life", the key credit comes from the €50K, not the two years.

Have you raised any investment already?
How much have you raised, and is there any significance to the investor? A client of mine once raised a modest sum from a former CEO of Mont Blanc, the manufacturer of exquisite, high-quality ink pens. Such an investment showed me that the startup must be of high quality too. The Mont Blanc guy surely wouldn't invest in something that wasn't of the highest level! Equally, if your investor has made previous commitments to significant companies, that adds credibility.

If there is no significance to the investor: no problem. Simply mentioning that others have already put money into your business gives a signal of reduced risk to a new investor.

How much are you raising now? Be specific.
The big question: Should I mention an actual figure? My answer is: Always! It's incredibly frustrating for an investor to hear a great pitch and not have clarity on the level of investment you are looking for. It suggests something is hidden, or you are not professional and don't know how much you need. Tell them a specific number and avoid being vague. Statements like, "Approximately 250-300K..." or "Around 500K...," give a message that the actual amount has not been thought through.

What will that money be used for? And what milestone will you reach?
Give three headline activities where the money will be spent. The challenge here is that you don't have time to tell in detail what you'll use it for, yet if you say noth-

ing, investors will feel you aren't serious. Usually your reply becomes a little generic – for example, "Develop our app, build the team and increase our sales/marketing push." This is sometimes the best you can do under time pressure.

You can however add some milestones to make your reply more specific. What will be the revenue next year? Will the money take you to a new level of users, or a new market or vertical? Share any steps forward that the investment will fuel to clarify the value it will have for your company and the impact for the investor.

Is there anything else you need?
Maybe you are looking for an investor with specific knowledge of a particular market, or who can introduce you to potential customers in a new industry. If so, be transparent about your needs. You might just get the help you're looking for if you put it out there.

Be choosy!
At the beginning of your investment hunt, you may simply be happy if any investor gives you the time of day. However, it's best to see this process as a marathon, not a sprint. Most funded startups talk to many investors – often more than 60 – before funds materialise. At a certain moment in that process, start getting more selective about whom you target. You want to make sure you don't waste your time, or anybody else's.

Here's an example of how that might all look: "We've invested €25K of our own money and received €75K from angel investors. We're now raising €650K, of which €150K is already committed. We'll spend this round on launching in country X, hiring two growth hackers and a sales leader, and hiring two developers to add function Y to the product. As a result of this investment, we expect to reach a turnover of €1,5 million by the middle of next year."

65

One thing not to mention in a public pitch is the deal – what percentage you offer in exchange for the money. That is always a matter of negotiation, and I would recommend discussing that face-to-face in a meeting, not in public.

For corporate innovation teams: What if your pitch is to the Board?

Translate "investment" into "what do you need?" Board members and decision makers need to learn from your pitch what investment you want: What will it take to make it happen and bring your idea into value for the company?

What they don't want to hear is vague mumblings about, "More time", "If we could get a bit more budget", "We're thin on the ground in terms of people" and, "Some support from you guys would really help." They need to know specifics, some quantifications, so they can make a yes-or-no decision without needing time to deliberate.

- How long do you need to reach which milestone?
- How much money is necessary and what milestone can you reach with it?
- Which additional roles are required to build up the team? Do you have particular people with relevant skills in mind?
- What sponsorship do you need from the top?

That last question is often the most critical of all. Someone in the Board backing you up and evangelising your work to the organisation can be the difference between success and failure, and surprisingly much more important than money and resources. If there is support from the Board, resources will come. With no sponsorship, a project has a high potential of failing.

66

More information
on milestones

Action – 15-minute task – Brainstorm your investment ask.

Write on Post-its®:

Startups:

1. Have you invested money yourselves? If yes, how much?
2. Have you raised money in the past? How much?
3. How much are you looking for now?

Corporate teams:

1. What time and people do you need in addition to money? Do you need a sponsor for the project?

Both:

1. What will you spend the money on?
2. What milestone will this investment help you reach?
3. What are the specifics about the types of investors you are looking for: how many? With specific experience, knowledge or network in a certain industry?

67

Team

If you ask any investor or Board member what the most important aspect of a startup is, they will automatically say, "team". It's almost a Pavlovian response. The team is the critical part of the startup and not the product or the business model.

There is plenty of truth in this answer, although we need to look a little deeper to understand what it truly means.

The truth is demonstrated by the reaction of an investor to a pitch we saw together.

He said to me afterwards: "The market's really interesting. Product? Terrible, but at least they've used it to engage with customers. Business model? Looks uncertain right now. I think they're on the wrong track there. But the team is really solid – I'm going to talk to them."

Think about that! Bad product, poor business model, yet follow-up from the investor. This is interesting because the pitch demonstrated that the team had identified a real problem in a large market and, most of all, was able to execute and get connected with customers. These two aspects of a startup are generally the weakest of all.

Chiefly, the strength of the team indicates how resilient you will be when trouble hits – as it surely will someday – and whether you have the skills to build, learn and grow the business. Anything that shows you are a strong unit reduces risk for the investor.

So how do you explain the value of your team? It's not easy, and often ends up in a lot of clichés, sounding a bit like this:

"Here's Bill – he's awesome! And here's Jill – she's awesome, too! And then there's Bob – he's the most awesome of awesome!"

None of these compliments help your cause! What you're looking for are one or two memorable points that stand out about the team. There are two major aspects you can focus on:

1. *Rational: Relevant experience and skills*
If your team members have worked for major brands or organisations, then mention that by showing the logos of those companies. If there are a lot of brands between you, mention the most impactful and relevant three companies.

Equally, if anyone of your team has won awards, has experience at an early stage of a certain industry, or is acclaimed in any other way, then mention it.

68

Another common and effective message is, "Between us we have over 10 years' experience in e-commerce," or "over 22 years of experience in retail among the team."

A key signal of less risk for an investor, is if you have co-founded a startup previously and had a successful exit. It's rare, but if this applies to you, use it as an unfair advantage. Be prepared, though, for the question: "If you've had a successful exit, why do you need investment?"

2. Non-Rational: What binds you together as a team, and what connects you as a unit to the problem you are solving
If you have a special and memorable connection among your team members, it can be a powerful reassurance to investors. It tells that you will survive difficult times together.

I often ask clients, more as a joke to illustrate my point: "Have you climbed mountains together?" "Yes! We have!", was the reply from the team from CrazyLister.

In their Demo Day pitch they showed a picture of the co-founders on the top of a snowy mountain. Message: "We know how to work together in extreme circumstances, and we don't give up."

Some companies I've coached were co-founded by family members. When they told this story in their pitch, the signal received by the audience was, "We will stick together."

Another CEO, Ronald Kouvelt of Stu-Comm, told: "I've known my co-founder for 25 years – and I'm just 27, so that's a large part of my life!" It made the audience smile, while delivering another 'we stick together' message.

Your product or service itself may also drive the kind of people involved. A team who created an app for separated parents and their children was co-founded by a group of parents. They were all experiencing problems of scheduling and communication as a result of their own breakup – and were able to bring in their

69

How to pitch to a
Board of Advisors

own highly credible knowledge of the problems parents in their situations face. This ability to relate helped them develop their product, and made a strong impression on investors.

It may be that you have assembled a team from various backgrounds, and there is no special bond. If that is the case, simply focus on the relevant experience and skills.

If you are a young team with limited experience, then focus on character and team bond.

Remember: there's never much time to talk about the team, so just try to focus on one or two aspects that may make your team stand out in terms of experience or character.

One further suggestion: it is an option to talk about your Board of advisors. If you have one, avoid detail. Briefly mention one or two members of that Board, who have very specific expertise that can help you reach the next level. This leverage can also add to your credibility.

70

Action – 15-minute task – Brainstorm your team.
Write on Post-its®:

1.   Who are the core team members?
2.   What rational elements should be told? Think of experience and skills.
3.   What about non-rational? Anything about your character? What binds you together, what's your shared mission?
4.   Are you long-time friends or family members? Have you worked in startups together before? Or have you worked together on projects for a company?
5.   What's the most surprising and memorable thing about your team?
6.   Is there a Board of Advisors? Who in that Board stands out as a person with skills or network that will propel you to the next level?

ACTION

Call To Action and End Statement

Pitches often close by tailing off with a rather lame mumble that trails off meekly: "Well that was it, I guess... so I'll finish... unless there are any questions...?"

That's a pity, because the last thirty seconds of your pitch is the first thing that they will think and feel about you as a business person and about your business as a proposition.

Wrapping up the pitch with a powerful and clear set of prepared sentences marks you as a professional, and someone who does his or her job 100 percent until the very end. Therefore, make a clear plan for what you will say. Here's my suggestion for how to finish it up.

Give them a quick summary of what they've seen, touching on three big points you want them to remember about your business.

Next, give a clear Call To Action. Look back at your objective: What was it you wanted to achieve in the first place with this pitch? And what do you want the audience to do straight afterwards: Download a free version of your app? Come and talk to you? Arrange an appointment? Take a survey? Or simply pass on your story? Ensure there is a clear first next step.

Finally, you could end with a reminder of who you are and what you do. Alternatively, you could finish with an 'I Believe' statement. Tell them, "I believe this is really important because..." and give them a final, short, one-sentence personal message about why it matters.

Here's an example of these three elements in action:

- What you've seen is that we're addressing a one-billion Euro problem, and have created significant traction

71

with our solution, thanks to an experienced and committed team.

- If you share our vision, come and talk to us after the pitches and let's arrange a one-hour follow-up meeting to discuss further.
- I believe our product will make a true difference to this industry, because it will bring people together. And that's what I personally stand for, connecting people.

72

Action – 10-minute task – Brainstorm your Call To Action and End Statement.
Write on Post-its®:

1. What is the Call To Action? Make it as solid and as actionable as possible.
2. How will you close your pitch? What are the final messages you want your audience to remember?
3. What is the first next step you want your audience to take?

Oh, one more thing... Why you?

You'll notice that this element is separate from the rest of the Pitch Canvas©, because answering Why you? can show up in any part of the pitch that fits.

I keep asking investors: "What do you want to see in a pitch?" The most consistent answer is: "I want to see the passion in the eyes of the entrepreneur. I want to see real commitment from the pitcher. I want to feel that they are truly in it for the long run."

Your audience questions many things when receiving your pitch, and one of the most critical points they are assessing is your personal drive to reach the targets you set yourself.

The quality of the team, the pain you fix, market size, product you develop, traction you create and business model

More on
Why you?

you use to earn money are all essential influences on their confidence too. Yet the final piece of the story is the person in front of them, the spokesperson of the team and its vision. Why should they believe you when you say, "We're going to change the world."? Why should they have confidence in you as a person?

The way to approach this is to ask yourself these questions:

- What do I believe in? What do I stand for?
- Why did I start this in the first place?
- Why do I love what I am doing?

Write down everything that comes to mind, and start to build a narrative of what your personal drive is all about.

One of the best ways to show that passion to your audience is to focus on values and beliefs. Answering the three questions above will help you get closer to building their confidence and growing their understanding of your true inner drive to succeed and deliver value to your customers.

What if you can't answer the Why you questions?

Maybe you're just a smart entrepreneur who has found a match for your knowledge and a major problem that people experience. You have no personal connection to the problem you are fixing or the people you fix it for. It's simply a way to live, to make money, to do something you enjoy.

If that is the case, then it may be best to be transparent about it. But before you are, use the two concepts below to question your motivation thoroughly and search for your possible answer to "Why you?".

1. Start with Why by Simon Sinek: The basic premise of Sinek's book and TED Talk: "If you're Dell, you make PCs, whereas if you're Apple, you're here to make a dent in the world." Dell would find it difficult to shift out of the world of PCs because its drive is to make great PCs. Apple effortlessly shifted into the worlds of music, phones and television, because

73

its internal and external driving force is about improving consumer experience.

Starting with Why is at a higher level, focused on problem solving and value for your audience, not on products. The Why is your higher purpose and the product is one of the ways you achieve your goals.

2. *The Five Whys:*
If you ask yourself why you do this – or better, get someone else to ask you – and you keep asking, "Why? Why is this important for me?", there will be a moment when you reach a deeper level of your true motivation. Keep asking why creating this business and building this product is important to you.

I've had entrepreneurs say to me, "My own story feels irrelevant. What they care about is the business." Yet, I've seen so many investors convinced by one deep insight into a person's motivation during a pitch, that I know it's worth spending time on motivation.

Think about it deeply. This really matters.

Put yourself on the line. Tell your audience why you believe this needs to happen, and why you are determined to succeed.

The amount of time you need for this task depends on how easily you can answer the question of "Why you?". Based on the ideas in this chapter, invest the time necessary to get closer to your own motivation. Watch Simon Sinek, do the Five Whys, read, discuss, and keep looking for the story of your true motivation.

Perhaps add: It's when you feel it on the inside that you have found the one of perhaps many reasons that make you passionate about your product.

74

Action – 15-minute task – Brainstorm your own purpose and Why you?

Imagine someone asks you, "Why are you doing this?" What would you say? Write down all possible answers, and look at it from different angles.

1. What's your personal motivation for solving this problem or creating this company? Is there a personal reason why you started this business?

2. Do you struggle with this problem personally and want to have it solved because you want the solution yourself?

3. What have been the turning points? What obstacles have you overcome, and what have been the best moments? When did you realise you might have a real shot at creating this company, and what did that mean to you?

1.2.3 Types of pitches

We have now discussed all the content that you could need for your pitch and the Q&A session afterwards. However, naturally there are some important content differences for certain pitches, depending on the situation, the audience and number of minutes available.

Investor pitch: preparing all the elements of the Pitch Canvas© will help you be ready. Once your audience is interested, they will follow up with questions about the metrics: retention rates, return user rates, cost of acquisition, average daily users, etc. Be prepared with this data, and if you have great figures, consider putting two or three of those points in the pitch.

Customer pitch: the biggest differences compared to an investor pitch, come at business model, investment and team.

- Business model – Customers will be more interested in pricing than your business model. Unless pricing is a significant differentiator, I advise always to keep the price out of the early-stage pitch and send proposals after the meeting. If you must mention it, give bandwidth; "A yearly contract usually costs between X and Y", so that you don't pin yourself to any agreement without further negotiation.

- Investment – While preparing, you can translate this into: "What do I want from my customer." That might be that they commit to a feasibility study, an agreement for a follow-up meeting, a signature or a cheque. In short, what do you want the customer to agree to?

- Team – Investors are deeply interested in the skills and character of individual team members. However, customers are more interested in the skills you have as a group. For example, for an investor pitch, you might say: "Jill, Jean and Bill have been committed to this industry for many years, because they are passionate about it." However, for a customer pitch, you would make it more generic: "As a

group, we have over twenty years of experience in this industry."

The customer is more focused on what you can deliver and less on who will do it. They just want to know what skills you have within your company and how these skills will add value to them. Investors understand that your product and the market may change in the future, and the ability of the entrepreneurs to adapt to that change is critical.

Management Board: The most important adjustment compared to a startup pitch to investors is to clarify why your proposal matters for your company. Will it help your company position itself as an innovator? Or address a gap in the company's offerings? Does the proposal match strategic changes in future plans, or enhance some initiatives already running in the company? Answering these questions shows you have looked at the issue from the perspective of the management team, not just from your own point of view.

Head of European start-up and scaleup ecosystem activities at PwC

Is pitching really important in large companies like PwC?

Just like startups, we're in a constantly changing environment and have to pitch many ideas to keep up with that change. We also need to win new business from clients and being able to pitch our purpose (*Building Trust in Society, and Solving Important Problems*). Being clear on the problem that we fix for clients, and how we fix it with our proposition, really matters. And time is of the essence! Clients have less and less time to listen to long stories.

We also have our own innovation processes. Our people have many ideas and a pitch pushes the idea creators to get clarity on what the actual problem is. Their pitch has to convince stakeholders that PwC is the right party to help with their important problems, and that the idea or proposed solution is strong enough for us to invest in as a company. In terms of both internal innovation and selling to our clients, pitching is crucial.

Is there a big difference between pitching an innovation idea in a big corporate and a startup pitching?

I don't see a big difference. The same elements are essential, such as what's the pain, what can you do to solve that pain, what's the business case, and what are the people skills and resources you need?

The difference comes in the ask for investment in a corporate innovation program. When pitching to the Board, you're often asking for a sponsor, people to put time into the project, or time for yourself to invest in validating the idea. But finally, you're asking for trust and help and that part is similar to asking an investor to put in money, network and industry knowledge.

77

The typical picture of a corporate presentation is long, 30 to 60 minutes, bullet points, loads of information. Is that still going on in large companies?
Yes, that is still happening. Often, that starts with large companies having branding policies and standard templates which people have to comply with. And these tend to be loaded with bullet points and lots of text. They don't always stimulate more creative ways of presenting because people start with the slides first.

When it comes to slides, it's truly a skill to present in a more visual way. A lot of people find it easier to read five bullet points than having an image and memorising what they need to say. Clearly though, a strong visual and a great explanation can make more impact than reading a few bullet points out!

The biggest issue for many corporates is that they are so inside-out. They become too focused on their own world, thinking that they know what the outside world wants, instead of looking to the customer and what they really need. Startups do this really well, following the Lean Startup principle.

Often, a large corporate comes up with an idea but there's no real validation with clients and therefore no proper understanding of the customer problem. You regularly see long presentations with what someone thinks is a great idea, and they are kind of disappointed if people ask the question: "Do you know if the market wants this?"

Startups appreciate that getting close to the detail and friction points of a customer journey, helps them identify true value. That's the background to a truly great pitch: Understanding the actual pain and demonstrating how your product solves it. You can only do that by being outside-in.

What grabs your attention in a pitch?
In terms of the style of pitch, it's the energy. How do they present, do I feel the passion, can I get the feeling that this person can really do it? If they are enthusiastic and committed, then I get enthused too.

When it comes to content, I am often grabbed by a smart formulation of the pain and a new angle to a problem that I had never thought of. As an example, I once saw these two Polish guys who had come up with a game for the Xbox which helped prevent backpain. The way they caught my attention was by showing that the #2 illness that causes absence at work is back pain, and I had no idea about that.

I went in with the mindset of: "Yes, I heard about it, they're doing this nice game, probably that helps people a bit." But then you hear the business impact their idea could have and it totally changes your thinking. That's how a pitch can open up the world of a specific important problem and makes you realise the possibilities.

How far can you actually get in a large company with pitching? Isn't the business case and documentation all that counts?
A great pitch can get you very far. Not only because of the quality of the pitch itself, but because of the what the preparation process forces you to do. You must think deeply about your idea and whether it is worth investing in, both from a company perspective and investing your own precious time in it.

The pressure of an audience listening critically to your pitch, causes you to question: Do you have the stamina to go through this whole process in a corporate environment? You'll have to evangelise and move decisions relentlessly, through what are often slow processes in a large company. This preparation helps you conclude whether you are truly committed to the idea, to say: "Yes, this IS what I want to do", and communicate that commitment.

Pitching forces the innovators to analyse their idea. Not just see it as something fun. To try and get some money, spend a bit of time on it. They need to commit and a pitch helps them to make that decision.

What's the toughest pitch you ever had to give?

The way that startups pitch, means they can test it out, get feedback and develop it. That's because the story at its core is the same every time and they have to do it again and again. They have the luxury of making those mistakes.

The pitches that I normally have to do are one shot only, while pitching for new business with clients. You choose an angle for your talk or pitch and the risk is always: Does this angle work or not? And if it doesn't, you're done! There is no second chance to pitch to a client for a project and that means every external pitch is exciting. You choose a story for why your company can do this best for the customer and how you differentiate. And either you nail it or you don't! ●

1.2.4 Putting the Pitch Canvas© into action

Once you've done the brainstorm exercises, take a new flipchart and draw the Pitch Canvas© on one page. Gather all your brainstorms and, section by section, place the Post-its® into each block, removing any that you think are irrelevant. Ensure that you've answered all the questions in each block, or if you don't have answers, make a note of that. It's good to know what you don't know!

Make sure you have at least three Post-its® per block (and ideally many more). Take more time to brainstorm again if anything feels incomplete.

This is not a one-time task. It's a good idea to revisit the Pitch Canvas© any time something changes in your business, or you feel the need to develop your pitch to the next level.

How do you turn content on the Pitch Canvas© into a pitch script?
The Pitch Canvas© is not intended to give you a script or a storyline straight away. Rather, it's a thinking and brainstorming tool that will take you closer to the story you want to tell. Completing it and thinking through answers to all the issues will give you the building blocks to prepare for any pitch. After completing the Pitch Canvas©, you will not have a script or a storyline, but you will have all the possible content that investors and influencers need to know about your business to be able to make a decision.

However, that content is not organised yet. Now you've gone through the brainstorm, it's time to create a storyline.

I'm regularly asked: "Should I tell my pitch in the order of the Pitch Canvas©?" My answer is: "No, not necessarily." You could start the pitch with the Pain or your personal Why you?, which connects you to the problem, and demonstrates how and why you are driven to solve this problem for customers. Equally, if you are not sure how to start, you can follow the Pitch Canvas© order of content to start with.

The key is to find a structure that suits you and that you feel comfortable with. Once again, to find the best structure for your pitch, Post-its® will serve you well.

1.2.5 Review your brainstorm and select the important points

Now that you have a lot of ideas written down, you need to review the brainstorm and start to identify which items you might finally talk about. Your goal is to create a storyline consisting of a number of chapter headings, and a few content blocks per chapter. Here's the process.

Take a step back, and look at each block of the Pitch Canvas©. Review your notes on the audience and the objective, and consider the amount of time available to pitch. These three will guide you on which and how much content you'll talk about. Then ask yourself: "What are the most important subjects for each block?"

For example, you have a three-minute pitch. What about the pain? You may have eleven Post-its® describing various aspects of the problem you're solving. Which two or three will you focus on in the pitch?

Then look at the product. Which of the Post-it® ideas capture the most important issues about your product and the way it solves the pain? What is essential to tell, and what is not so important?

Continue through all the blocks and start to highlight which items you might talk about in your pitch. Remove anything you think has less relevance or you don't have time to tell.

You can do the highlighting by rearranging the Post-its®, using another colour pen to mark the items you think are most important. This is a selection process where you need to force yourself to narrow down to the essentials.

A lot of teams find this part really difficult. They want to tell everything! But with limited time, you need to be ruthless and make a selection.

A way to approach it is to force yourself to have a maximum of three things you'll talk about per block of the Pitch Canvas©. Imagine you have only 30 seconds to talk about each piece. What would you focus on?

Create Chapter Headings For Your Pitch

It's time to extract some structure and a storyline from your brainstorm. Take a separate piece of flipchart paper, and start to organise your selected Post-its® into chapter headings and content.

Here's how to do it.

Start to place Post-its® as chapter headings. These could be titles from the Pitch Canvas©. For example, start with pain. Next, add the part about Why you?, then maybe the product you created. Follow that with the traction of who is already buying, the Product Demo, What's Unique, and so on.

After you build the outline of the pitch in chapters, you can start to add the content pieces that you highlighted as important. As you do this, start to say your pitch out loud, Post-it® by Post-it®. This process will help you begin to find the words and phrases to capture what you really want to tell.

As you add content and say it out loud, you will naturally find the flow that works for you. There are no rules about what should come first and what order to follow, although I would advise to get the pain very clear at an early stage. Other than that, feel free to move the chapters around until it feels right.

It's up to you. No two pitches will – or should – ever be the same. This brainstorming process is designed to give you the best framework to find your story, and ensure you cover all the essentials.

1.2.6 **To script or not to script**

Yes! You're done brainstorming. You know exactly what information you want to share during your pitch. Now you need to find the right words to create that perfect script.

I recommend startups to script their pitch for anything up to seven minutes. Writing it out word for word and memorising the script. This is not always well-received however, and you may have some of the following objections that I regularly hear:

"If I script it, I won't be spontaneous."
"I can't follow a script, it means I can't improvise."
"It will feel fake if I script, I just want to be myself."

Some years ago, when I worked at a large company, I would have said the same. In those days, it was not unusual to give a presentation of nearly an hour. These presentations are hard to memorise, you have less time pressure and expectations are a little different.

When it's a pitch, the audience have very high expectations. There is often a time limit of one, three or five minutes, and there is no time to lose. Audiences expect it to be well-prepared and straight to the point, with no wasted time. Investors and Board members are busy and want you to get into the story, get through it and get finished, so they can make their decisions.

Over the last few years, I've seen thousands of pitches, and I see what happens to the ones who don't memorise their scripts. The pressure of expectation is simply too great, and they crumble almost every time.

Especially the ones who want to improvise and be spontaneous fail. They spend too many seconds on less important issues, run out of time and end up forgetting to tell the most important points about their business.

Making a pitch is like having 25 applications open at once. You are doing an incredible number of things when in front

84

of an audience: Thinking about what to say next, how to say it, where to stand, how to use your hands, checking whether the audience likes it. Which slide comes next, which words to emphasise, when to pause, when to click – have I made eye contact with everyone? It's a miracle anyone manages to get a word out!

If you add data retrieval to the mix, there is a massive chance of a meltdown. Like a computer, the human brain can crash when it can't find the data it needs and there is no computing – or brain – power available.

It might sound counter-intuitive, but my experience is that memorising a script is the key to spontaneity and authenticity. If you know your story 100 percent, you are able to focus completely on how you engage your audience, and not on what you want to say.

I've seen this happen countless times. Throughout the process of developing the pitch, there is a constant element of uncertainty. The brain keeps questioning, even as you speak: "Is this the story I really want to tell?" However, once a pitcher finalises a script, the questioning stops. This *IS* the story they want to tell, and as they memorise it, an element of certainty builds. Once they memorise the script exactly, the body language starts to fall into place, and confidence grows.

The real secret is to have enough time between memorising the story and giving the pitch to make the story your own. You need at least a couple of days to identify what words matter most in the story, and how you are going to emphasise them with voice, body and energy. We talk a lot more about this in the Deliver section of this book.

In short, making a great pitch is very little about inspiration and very much about following a smart process and doing the work. That work is wrapped up finally by the memorising of the script, and a lot of practice to make it great.

85

Examples of
openings

Now that you're ready to put your brainstorm into a script to memorise, the question is, how can you sharpen the elements of your pitch so that the big highlights grab attention, convince the audience, and get them to take action?

1.3 OPEN, THREE AND CLOSE

1.3.1 First impressions count or confuse. How to open your pitch

It's a critical moment of your pitch – the opening. You need to start with power and precision to convince your audience that the information is relevant to them and they should definitely listen further.

Going through the process of identifying who you're pitching to will help you decide how to adapt your opening to the interests of your listeners.

First, let's look at what goes wrong time and again. Picture the typical opening of a presentation or pitch. The pitcher shuffles into place and starts to ramble.

"Good morning ladies and gentlemen... Oh, sorry, it's afternoon, isn't it? Haha, well, erm, thanks so much for the opportunity to tell you my story here today, on this wonderful stage, and it's great to see so many familiar faces and people who have come from so far... Well, I guess I should introduce myself... I'm Steve Smith, assistant to James Bream who is the head of the division off..."

You get the picture. At least 30 to 40 seconds of meaningless introduction without any hint of content or value for the audience, and no clear statements about why they should listen.

During one pitch competition I attended, the pitches were two minutes long and twenty percent of the pitchers began pretty much like I just described! As a result, they devoted one third of their pitches to... well, to nothing.

This happens a lot. Why does a strong opening matter? Does it really make such a difference?

86

Instant judgments

In the first milliseconds of your pitch the audience has all kinds of judgments in their heads. Most are subconscious and based on one essential fact: as human beings, we hate complexity.

Every piece of information presented to you is filtered by your wish for simplicity and your basic subconscious questioning of everything around you. *Is this valuable to me? Will this help me understand the world around me? Will I get an opportunity if I invest time and energy listening to this? Is this new information or have I seen it before and there's no need to bother with it?*

If you don't trigger your audience in the right way during the first seconds of your pitch, you will lose them. After the typical rambling first 20 seconds of a pitch, a signal is sent to the audience's minds: *This seems irrelevant, there's no value here. Ignore!*

If you take a long time to tell what you are doing or have a long-winded introduc-tion, the audience will switch off. They don't know why this pitch is going to help them.

If you open with complexity, with a lot of numbers or with a lot of details on the slides, and the audience gets confused and switches off. Rolling out graphs, end-less facts or detailed process flows causes the same reaction.

The classic nine-bullet point agenda slide, followed by sentence after sentence typed onto the following slides, causes the audience to think: *I have seen these kinds of pitches before. It was terrible last time, I'm sure it will be terrible again. Ignore!*

This is pretty devastating news, because if you look back at the last ten presenta-tions or pitches you've seen, you can surely remember many openings like these. Since audiences are switching off so often, it means that many presenta-tions and pitches are a **complete waste of time.**

Open with intrigue

In the opening seconds, the task is to create two triggers in the minds of the audience. Firstly, "I am listening to a professional." And secondly: "This story sounds interesting – tell me more." There are several ways to achieve this.

1. **State the pain and how you fix it.** "Can you imagine, we spend 20 minutes every time we look for a parking space? Can you believe 30 percent of all traffic jams in major cities are caused by people looking for parking? And can you imagine we spend over one year of our lives parking our car? We're Mobypark, and we're here to make parking cheaper, easier and fun."

   The pain is instantly quantified in a way that resonates with and intrigues the audience. There's a clear statement of the industry the startup is working in and its ambition in 57 words, which takes around 22 seconds to tell.

2. **Open with a question.** "Who here likes to fill out their taxes? We're Taxbutler, and we make filing your taxes a 20-minute, pleasurable task, instead of a chore that takes hours."
   By asking a question, the audience is immediately engaged in the subject, and your value is quantified in the first 15 seconds.

   Note: If you want a response from the audience, the question needs to be worded and managed very carefully. Make the question answerable in only two ways, yes or no, and show them what they have to do by holding your hand up, or asking them to shout the answer out loud. (More on this on page 96.)

3. **Start with an experience story.** "Two years ago, we had a company selling accessories for the iPhone. We noticed everyone was playing a game called Draw Something. We thought, wouldn't it be easier to draw with a stylus than with your finger?

88

So we created a Groupon promotion and planned to sell 200 items. But you know what? We sold 3000! Great sales, but then we had a problem. We had to create 3000 shipping labels which took us 60 hours to copy and paste our customer data into the shipping company's system. We thought, there must be a better way to do this for webshops like us, and we looked for a solution, but we couldn't find it. That's when we created SendCloud."

This is a longer approach: 122 words and around 50 seconds. It was the introduction of a seven-minute pitch and the time is well spent. It creates a short, memorable story that illustrates the problem very clearly. However, this way takes a minute to get to the point where you talk about your company. And one of the most golden pieces of advice for any pitch is to ensure you tell who you are and what you do within the first 20 to 30 seconds of the pitch.

That's why, in this case, SendCloud started their pitch with the following before telling the experience story: "Hi, I'm Rob, CEO of SendCloud. We connect webshops with shipping carriers, and we're already working with companies like DHL." With this approach, the pitch is positioned in a way that tells the audience: "This is the problem we fix and we're already succeeding." The audience is then ready to listen to a story that explains why this is a problem. Without this initial framing, there was a danger that the audience wouldn't understand the relevance of the story.

4 **Just get straight into it.** "Hi, I'm David Beckett, I'm a pitch coach, and I'm here to ensure your ideas have a voice. Let me share with you why it's so hard to pitch and how I help startups make investment winning pitches, with online learning tools." Such an opening tells who you are, what you do, the value and change

89

you bring and your insight into the theme of the pitch – in just 42 words and in less than 20 seconds.

There is no single perfect way to open. What is certain is that you need to be professional, concise and clear. Make a conscious decision of what you will say, and practice those first sentences again and again.

Your first 20 to 30 seconds are the highest stress moments possible for you as a presenter, and knowing exactly what you will say is one of the best ways to manage that stress and turn it into action. (More on page 181.)

1.3.2 **Think it through, write it down, say it out loud, get feedback**

How do you know if you have an effective opening to the pitch? By brainstorming your story on Post-its®, you succeeded in getting the story out of your head. Now, before pitching, try this exercise: a simple, yet extremely powerful method of testing that will transform the whole pitch, and is especially useful for the opening.

The following is one of the most powerful exercises to develop your pitch to the highest level.

Most people prepare slides for hours and hours and present them. They take no time to test what they are going to tell by saying it out loud. The story simply goes from their heads, to the slides, to the audience.

For 99 percent of pitchers it is impossible to succeed like this. You need to *hear* the story out loud to find out if it sounds right to you. You'll find that by saying it out

Action – 15-minute task – Write down and test out your opening.

1. Go back over your brainstorm (see page 82) and make notes on what would be the most powerful opening three sentences. What will be the way to capture the audience's attention and make a professional opening to the pitch?
2. Write down your three opening sentences.
3. Find somebody to test the opening sentences with out loud. Ask them to listen and give the following specific feedback:
    a. Is this opening professional?
    b. Does this opening make them want to find out more?
    c. Can they give a friendly piece of advice for improving the opening?

loud you can refine the words you use to explain the points you want to get across.

It's equally important to have others hear your pitch and give feedback. Naturally there are many opinions among your listeners, and it's good to find out how different people react to what you say before you make the big pitch.

When you do this exercise, one of three things can happen.

1. You say your opening sentences and may think, "Well, that sounds a bit stupid!" When you write things down on paper, you intend the words to be read, not heard. Written language is more formal than spoken language. When you say it out loud, the written words may feel very unnatural. If

this happens (as it does for around 50 percent of my clients!) then rewrite the words in line with how you speak in daily life.

2. You say the three sentences and think that they are clear. However, the person in front of you looks as if you just explained quantum theory badly. Ask what is wrong, what is not clear? How could you make it clearer? Then rewrite the opening sentences based on the feedback, and test again.

3. You say the sentences, and your test audience is nodding. It seems they *get it*.

In any of the three cases, keep asking the same questions in terms of feedback. Is it professional, and does it make them want to know more? What don't they understand? What would help to make it clearer? The refinements you make to your opening through this process will elevate the first seconds of your pitch immensely.

Apply this approach to test any part of your pitch

You can go through these steps for any part, or all of the parts, of the pitch. Break it down into pieces and find someone to test it out with. For example, tell a colleague or a friend: "I want to explain the problem we are fixing. Can you tell me if the pitch is strong enough and understandable?"

Think it through; write it down; say it out loud; get feedback. Then adjust based on the feedback, and repeat!

The more you do this, the more likely your pitch will resonate with your audience.

1.3.3 Make your message easy to absorb: The Power of Three

The next step is to begin to develop your storyline based on your brainstorm.

You'll find you want to tell a lot and express all the details of the great work you and your team are doing. However, the audience can't absorb all those details. Plus, as we've already seen, a pitch is all

about the highlights and getting the audience to want to find out more.

How do you define those highlights? This is where the Power of Three comes in: It helps you identify and communicate the most important parts of your overall pitch, as well as explain individual points simply and effectively.

But first, why is it three? Why not four or two?

Why is three so powerful?
Surprise, surprise, there are three main reasons.

   1. *The threes are all around us.*
Ready, steady, go. Lights, camera, action. Veni, Vidi, Vici. The Three Musketeers. Bronze, silver, gold. Beginning, middle, end.

Threes are everywhere and are also used by the biggest companies in the world. Here are a few examples.

When Apple launched the iPad pro, they simply positioned it as: Thin. Light. Epic.

TED.com currently features three main talks at the head of its main page. Dropbox communicates "Better, Safer, Together" for its business service.

Even humour works in threes! In England, we have numerous silly jokes about the Englishman, the Scotsman and the Irishman.

The reason? When we tell a joke, it is part of the ancient oral tradition of passing on information verbally, which existed before the invention of printing. When we tell a joke, we have to remember it, otherwise it fails.

We also want the listener to be able to pass the joke on and tell it to others. Breaking things into threes is the most effective way of making it memorable, for the person selling an idea and the listener.

93

Applying this principle to a pitch, you need to remember the pitch when telling it, and your audience needs to be able to pass it on. This process becomes so much easier when they get presented information in groups of three.

2. *Three is the smallest number with complexity.*
Earlier in the book, I mentioned that complexity is the enemy. Yet you don't want the audience to think this is all too easy. Telling in twos feels too flat and unresearched. Telling in threes gives an extra dimension.

Three is enough to give a feeling of depth, without overwhelming the audience.
It tells them you've done the work, but keeps the details to a minimum.

3. *There is a rhythm to three.*
Telling in threes simply feels right. "It's faster, easier, and most of all, it's cheaper." Try saying this out loud, and you'll find the emphasis will come naturally. The rhythm of three just works.

94

How do you apply the Power of Three?
Go through the following three exercises and you'll begin to apply the Power of Three instantly to your pitch.

Action – 15-minute task – Putting the Power of Three into action.

1. Go back over your pitch and think to yourself: If I could tell only three things, what would they be?

   These could be problem, solution and timeline. Or they could be the way the world used to be, how things changed, and how you enable people to adapt. Or the three issues could be your product, your traction and your team. Force yourself to break it down to only three key elements, the ones you definitely do not want to forget to mention.

   Once you've identified the three that really matter, write them down.

2. Take one of those items – your product, your traction, your team, What's Unique, or whichever you like – and break that one item down into three parts.

   For example, our product is about speed, convenience and engagement. Write these three things down. Now write one sentence per item.

Let's say: "The product is fast because we enable users to reach their goals in one third of the speed, thanks to machine learning. It's more convenient because…" et cetera.

3. Is there a way to tell your whole pitch in three words? Doing so may sound unusual at first, and it is not essential, but if you can do it, then it can be a great way to make your story memorable. It works especially for very short pitches at network events, in competitions or classic elevator pitches.

   For example: when I talk about Pitching, it all comes down to: Script, Design, Deliver. I could talk for days about this subject! But finally, I make sure that people remember the formula: Script, Design, Deliver.

   It doesn't have to be only three words; it could be three small groups of words. "Creates wealth, reduces cost, connects people," for example.

   Write down your story in three words or in three small groups of words.

95

1.3.4 Mastering the art of asking questions in a pitch

Raising a question is a great way to increase attention amongst the audience, yet it often goes badly wrong.

For example, the pitcher asks: "How many of you have experienced the feeling of...?" A few of the audience put their hands up, a few say quietly, "Me", but most feel unsure of what they should do. After almost no response, the pitcher has to fill in the gap, and it's all just a bit awkward...

This situation occurs because the pitcher has left it unclear to the audience how to express their opinions. The best way to ask questions is to give the audience clear guidance by making questions either rhetorical or digital.

Rhetorical: a question where you ask and give the answer yourself.

You might make a statement such as, "The problem is clear, and it's a multi-billion Euro pain. Here's our solution, using blockchain." However, turning this into a rhetorical question creates more focus. "The problem is clear and it's a multi-billion Euro pain. So what's our solution? Well, we put blockchain to work."

Why is this question more powerful than the statement? It's because the brain cannot receive a question passively. As humans, we are programmed to find solutions, starting from our first primitive origins. In fact, our ability to solve problems sets us aside from animals, and is one of the reasons we survived as a race.

This solution-finding reaction is triggered when we are asked a question, even if we know it is rhetorical. A statement can be something we disagree with, but a question invites us into a problem and then provides us the solution. It's a powerful way to bring the listener's attention to a peak.

Digital: a question with only two possible responses, and you show your audience how to express their response.

96

You could say in your pitch, "What do you think of data privacy?" This question leaves it open and there are a huge variety of possible responses in the minds of the audience. As a result, they don't know what they should do physically – speak, put their hands up, stand up – and both the pitcher and the audience are no better off.

If the pitcher switches to a digital question, she would say, "Who believes data privacy is important? Put your hand up if you do." There are only two options – hand up, or hand down. The pitcher can be certain that there are only two possible outcomes, and be prepared to follow-up on either response from the audience: lots of hands up, or a few.

This clarity creates a feeling that the pitcher is in control, and the audience feels comfortable with their part in the pitch.

1.3.5 Hear this! Make an announcement
One of the best ways to inject energy into your pitch is to announce something new.

Usually this energy would be something related to traction: a new deal with a major customer, a milestone in terms of users, a launch of a new product or service or an award or competition win.

This approach works especially well if you are pitching to a larger group, because if you do it correctly, the audience will clap. Applause always increases energy and creates a general feeling of positivity among the audience – on top of the fact that you are sharing a genuine breakthrough in your business.

If you do have something to announce, here is a selection of ways to do it.
- "My team and I have been working day and night to reach a new level of customers, and I am proud to share that just yesterday, we reached that new level: 10,000 users!"
- "We've been working hard to bring onboard our launching customer, and I'm delighted to share that our launching partner will be – Supermarket Y!"

97

- "Our technology has been gathering attention from some major companies, and that's led to us signing a great deal with a new technology partner. It's – Tech Z!"
- "I am proud to announce that we just signed a deal with the biggest bank in the Philippines – Bank X!"

The one constant in each of these approaches is to save the most important point for the end. Doing this creates a little tension, and the audience is curious to know who or what it is. When you announce a name at the very end of the announcement – with a small pause before telling the name and delivering with some energy and emphasis – there is a natural tendency for the audience to clap.

But, you may wonder, what if they don't clap? Don't worry, you can ensure that they do! If members of your team know the moment when you will make the announcement and want the audience to clap, they can applaud first. This will certainly cause the rest of the audience to join in.

One key point. Make sure you don't overdo it! Deliver one or a maximum of two announcements in this style, and spread them out across the pitch if there are two.

Equally, make sure the breakthrough is worth an announcement style of approach. If the audience doesn't feel what you focus on is a real breakthrough, then even if they clap, they will feel tricked into it. The purpose is to trigger them into realising you have made a genuine jump in your business. They give applause and feel it is justified.

Bear in mind that this announcement could be different every time you pitch, or at least, it should change regularly. Announcements need to be fresh to make an impact, and some members of the audience could hear you present on different occasions. If you doubt whether the announcement is fresh enough, it's better to remove it from the pitch than repeat

> *Action – 10-minute task – The announcement.*
> 1. Look at your business and see whether something has happened in recent days or weeks that could be worthy of an announcement.
> 2. Write out the way you would like to pitch the announcement.
> 3. Say it out loud, and make sure you position the key fact at the end of the sentence.

it and have half the audience thinking, "What? I've heard this before!"

1.3.6 How to close memorably and professionally

Just like the opening, the closing is critical. The last 20 seconds have a major influence on what the audience thinks of you and your business on a rational level, and what they *feel* about you as an entrepreneur and professional, on a non-rational level.

We've already found the closing of many pitches to be very poor, as if the pitcher hadn't thought about what he or she would say in those last few seconds.

Quite often, you hear something along the lines of, "Well, that's it, I guess... erm... I hope you enjoyed it, and, erm... I hope I could convince you of..." And the pitch trails off with a weak, "Any questions?"

This type of ending is like telling the audience, "I'm the type of person who does his work 90 percent." And nobody wants to work with 90 percent-ers, we all want to work with 100 percent-ers! Present yourself as a professional who does the work at the highest quality until the very last second.

You achieve this level of quality by making conscious decisions about the words and the last two to three sentences you will say to finish off the pitch. The ending could be a summary of what they have seen – especially referring back to the Power of Three content you have written down – followed by a Call To Action, so that it is clear what they should do as a first next step. Finally, remind them who you are and what you do. It could look something like this.

100

"What you've seen is that Ecodrive is cost-effective, sustainable and most of all, incredibly easy, thanks to a unique Mobile UX. Download our app now. We'd love to hear what you think after the pitches. We're EcoDrive, and we're bringing sustainable, instant driving to the world. Thank you!"

This closing reminds the audience of the value the business brings, gives a clear Call To Action and keeps the company firmly in mind to the last seconds.

Notice the one small, yet very important element of the closing, saying, "Thank you!"

The purpose of this essential signal is to tell the audience the exact moment the pitch has finished, so they know exactly when to clap. It's not about saying, "Thank you for your attention." After all, they should be listening, because you've got great stuff to tell!

You saying, "Thank you", is purely an end signal. The audience will clap in unison, and the collective feeling among the audience is that this has been a high-quality pitch, well rounded off by a true professional.

1.3.7 Finish on time

Almost every pitch is time-pressured. You'll be given a time limit such as five minutes, three minutes or even one minute, and usually this means that amount of time and not a second more!

Pitches often happen in a series and sometimes a jury or the innovation Board has to listen to over 20 pitches in a day. It's not surprising they want the story to be short!

I've listened to so many pitchers share their frustrations at this. "I never have enough time to tell all the details I want to tell!" I'm always sympathetic, yet realistic. The fact is, when a time limit is given there is a clear signal from the organisers on behalf of the audience for the pitch. They are telling the pitcher: "Give us the headlines first. We'll decide if we want the details later."

Whether the time available feels like it's enough or not, the rules are the rules. You are simply expected to finish within the time!

ACTION

Action – 10-minute task – Write down and test out your closing.
1. Go back over your brainstorm on Post-its® and think about what would be the most powerful closing three to four sentences. What will be the best way to wrap up the pitch professionally? What Call To Action do you want to give? And what's the most important thing you want them to remember about you and your business? In short, how can you make a truly professional closing to the pitch?
2. Write down your three to four closing sentences.
3. Just as with the opening, find somebody to listen to your closing sentences and ask them to give you the following specific feedback:
    a. Is this closing professional?
    b. Is it clear what your listener needs to do?
    c. Does this closing make them want to find out more?

And what happens if you don't? When the clock stops ticking, you'll be asked to stop, regardless of whether you have finished what you wanted to say. Or if there is no clock and you overrun your time, the audience will not appreciate the extra time taken and feel you are unprofessional. It's almost like saying, "I believe my time is more valuable than yours."

How do you manage the time? The first step is the script: make sure you don't write more than 140 words per minute. Humans can listen at a maximum of 150 words per minute. Speaking at a speed of more than 150 words per minute means the audience will find it difficult to follow large pieces of your pitch. Delivering at around 130-140 words per minute will enable you to inject enough speed to communicate energy, and still leave some space for pauses.

Secondly, practice against the clock. Say the whole thing out loud, at pitch speed, and see how long it takes you. If you are struggling to finish within the time

available, the only option is to cut content, otherwise you will be too stressed to succeed.

For example, if you have a three-minute pitch and you keep finishing around 02:56-02:59, you might feel you'll easily be able to finish within the time limit when the day of the pitch comes around. But if you stumble on a couple of words, you'll feel the pressure to speed up and finish quicker. This will result in a hurried message and a less natural delivery.

Ensure you are able to consistently to finish at least 5 to 10 seconds under the time limit in practice. Make a note about how you tend to deliver in a real pitch – faster, or slower than in practice? That will tell you how much time you are likely to take on the big day.

1.3.8 How to prepare for Demo Day or any other big pitch

You've gone through all the brainstorming, and you're sharpening and improving your story into a great script. You're becoming more certain of the message and getting clarity on what really matters. You're ready to make a professional, well-structured and organised pitch.

Yet, all of this is not enough. You need to go through the following steps: What, Decide, Memorise and Deliver. This will help you feel more certain about the pitch and you'll make the story your own.

We've been going through the What-process in this first section of this book, identifying the possible content of what to say. This step takes a long time, brainstorming all aspects of your business, testing it all out loud, and asking each other, "Do we say *this*, or should we focus on *that*?"

At a certain moment, this questioning needs to be turned into decisions about what you will say for that Demo Day or that final pitch to the Board. Deciding means finalising the script, which you ideally wrap up long enough ahead of the pitch, to allow time for the last two steps: Memorise and Deliver.

If you make the decisions about the storyline the night before, there is not

The four stages of turning a pitch script into your own story

®David Beckett 2017

enough time to get the pitch firmly in your head. Parts of it will flow, and other parts will feel like you're trying to remember what to say. You will feel this, and the audience will most definitely sense it too.

To create certainty, you need some days to memorise the pitch and to practice with your slides. In case you have recurring doubts about your authenticity if you memorise the pitch, look back at "To script, or not to script" on page 84, for why it works.

104

Make sure to plan backwards from the time of the pitch and set yourself a deadline for when you will finalise the script to at least 95 percent. My suggestion: do this at least a week before the big day for a make-or-break pitch. If it's less important, two to three days may be enough.

Focus initially on memorising the pitch. Print the script and say it all out loud, again and again, until you don't have to think before telling it. Quick ways to help you memorise include:

- Record the pitch and listen back while traveling in your car, on your bike, on public transport or while you exercise.
- Break the pitch into three parts. Sometimes practice only the last part, then just the middle, and sometimes only the beginning. This helps you gain confidence that you know what's coming next.
- Say your pitch out loud while standing up and pacing backwards and forwards, gesturing with your hands to emphasise important points. Although pacing during the pitch is not a good idea (check the Deliver section to learn why), it's proven that while trying to memorise, pacing increases retention.

Once the script is firmly in your mind, you can move on to the final step: Deliver. Section three of this book is all about how to present with certainty and passion, and will help you use your body language and voice to connect with your audience on various levels.

Most of all, as you practice your delivery, keep asking yourself: What do I really mean with these words? What fact do I want the audience to remember? What emotion do I want them to feel? These questions will help you put your focus and energy where it needs to be so that the attendees understand your message clearly.

To be able to practice the delivery of your 95 percent completed pitch, you need to have the slides ready. That's why we're going to work on Design next and Delivery last.

Let's look at how the visuals help elevate your well-structured script, boosting your connection with the audience, building your confidence and positioning you as a true pitch professional!

INTERVIEW SEAN PERCIVAL

Silicon Valley investor in over 120 startups, former director of leading US Accelerator 500 Startups

Tell me about your pitch model, the Traction Sandwich.

1. Traction
2. Problem
3. Solution
4. Team
5. Repeat Traction

The Traction Sandwich is a way to catch someone's attention. If you start the pitch with sales success, it gets the audience more interested. It shows you have a lot of validation and they will be more likely to listen to the rest of the pitch. If you start off with something too soft, or that doesn't tell what you're doing, or doesn't show validation, your audience is likely to be less interested and perhaps not even listen.

It's a sandwich because we start with traction and we also end with traction. As you leave the stage, even if they don't understand the economics, or the nuances of the business, they know that you have numbers and success, which means it's worth approaching you and finding out more about the business.

You see a lot of pitches, so what is it that causes you to say: "Hey, I should go and engage with these guys?"
I'm always looking for someone who pitches with passion. I'm also looking for someone who is solving a pain point that they've experienced themselves. I believe those founders create the best solutions, because they've been there before. They know the industry and they're not just creating another Uber because it's hot and trendy. They're solving a real problem that they as a person truly identify with.

Beyond that, it's traction, traction, traction, and especially momentum in that traction. For example, I love to see a company that's growing 20 percent month

106

over month for the last three months, because it shows me that something is happening. It doesn't matter if the baseline is small, growth shows there is validation and momentum in the business.

What role does pitching play in the journey towards getting funded?
Pitching is a bit of a 'dog and pony show' as we say in America. Most great founders don't pitch, they just grow their business. Even so, it is required because I think of it as lead generation. For example, you're speaking to an audience or a panel and with a great pitch you're getting them interested enough that they'll give you their business card. Then you can follow-up and have a real meeting.

Funding doesn't happen straight after pitching. People don't walk up and write cheques right after a pitch, or at least that's pretty rare! But get me interested with your story and then I'll be happy to have a call, spending 30 to 60 minutes going through more details of the business. If it sounds solid, we'll go on from there. In short, pitching is a clear way to get to that first meeting with a potential investor.

How do you see this statement from another investor I spoke to? "The pitch is dead. We've seen too many pitches, I'd rather have a talk with someone than be pitched."
There's some truth in that. There are too many Demo Days, there are too many founders who are good up there on stage, but are not good at shipping product. I am kind of sick of seeing founders win awards for pitching when they haven't even launched their product.

If you haven't gone out there, talked to customers, got a little bit of traction, you should be working on that, instead of practicing for the pitch.

In the end, there are only two kinds of pitches in the world. There's the Vision pitch and the Traction pitch. You can imagine which one attracts more funding. The Vision pitch is very difficult and the Traction pitch works. Work on getting traction first before you waste too much time getting on stage.

How about the difference between pitching in Europe and pitching in America?

In Europe, everyone's too damn modest. They undersell themselves. And Americans oversell themselves! The problem is, investors in America are used to entrepreneurs overselling. As a result, they will discount 20 percent of what you say and assume the truth is a little smaller than in your pitch. If you go to an American investor with a modest pitch, they will still assume the reality of the story is smaller than the way you are pitching it. You need to push yourself up, brag a little and not be so modest.

Also in Europe, people are a lot more shy when talking about traction. They are often worried that they only have a little bit of revenue and therefore don't want to talk about it because they feel it's not enough to be mentioned. But even that little bit of validation is enough and is worth talking about. Many startups have no sales or customers, so even small success is worth mentioning. It shows the first signs of take-up by the market and builds credibility.

In short, an American pitch is usually over the top, bragging, almost annoying. The European pitch is more modest, very soft, low energy. Investors put money into conviction, so if you don't have energy and passion, we're probably not going to invest. ●

DESIGN.

TWO

2.1 THE POWER OF VISUAL STORYTELLING

There are times when you need to pitch without slides, but on most occasions some visual support is required. And in most cases a slide deck will help you emphasise your key points.

As explained, start creating visuals only after you've brainstormed the storyline thoroughly, and have written your script. That way you focus on how to bring the story to life visually, rather than getting caught up in what you will say on the day.

In this section, you'll get the tools and resources that will help you make easy decisions about design, save you time and increase clarity. This chapter is intended for non-designers, and provides easy to apply approaches that professional designers use to create great slides.

Make the exercises work for you by taking a slide deck you already have, or a few slides you are working on, and applying the exercise tasks immediately. This way you can put the principles to work on your very next pitch.

But first, do you really need slides?

2.1.1 Should you use slides? Why visual storytelling matters

The basic principle of presenting with slides is to involve two senses instead of one. You're speaking and showing something on the screen at the same time. This means your audience is more likely to understand your message and remember the key points.

A slide deck using PowerPoint, Keynote, Prezi or any of the increasing number of alternatives available, is most commonly used. However, there may be situations where you can use other types of visuals. Whiteboard presentation has become popular in some companies, and using a pre-prepared flipchart with drawings and key words can also work with a small group.

111

Another approach is to have a graphic recorder capture the story on one big poster, which you can walk people through.

Nevertheless, for sheer portability and for having a format that people are used to receiving, a slide deck is the best approach.

What desperately needs to change though, is the way slides have been created for decades. Line after line of text, many bullet points, too much information crammed onto one slide, with a text point size that anyone more than two metres away will never be able to read.

Adding charts, multiple fonts and headache-inducing animation creates a recipe for boredom, confusion, and a failed message. This content overload has very little to do with what I recommend, to *support* your story, *visually*.

I believe the biggest reason why presenters don't change this crammed-full style of slides is not lack of will. I believe it's their lack of tools. Very few people are trained in design, yet we are expected to make slides as if we were.

Luckily these tools aren't complicated, and the first is how to turn text information into visuals.

2.1.2 60,002 reasons why visuals work better than words

The human brain processes visual information 60,000 times faster than text.

I'll give you a few moments to absorb that information, because it takes our mind some time to process words and concepts like this.

Yes, the brain makes instant associations with visuals, and takes more time to make sense out of words. As Daniel Kahneman shared in his book *Thinking, Fast and Slow,* as soon as we see an image, we get a feeling. We start to make lightning-fast associations from just that one visual. However, with text we have to work through the words to discover connections and context, and this is a longer process. About 60,000 times longer!

On top of this comes reason #60,001, visual information directly enters the long-term memory. We are much more likely to remember an image a week after a pitch than some carefully crafted, yet instantly forgettable bullet point sentences.

And here's reason #60,002. Of the content presented, we remember 20 percent of what we read and 80 percent of what we see.

In short, if you'd like to make it much easier and quicker for the audience to get connected to your story, make slide decks visual. Use images and icons to express concepts and ideas, and use a few key words rather than full sentences.

113

Over the coming chapters I'll share numerous ways to turn your text into visuals, and provide you with free image and icon sources.

If you have a nagging doubt, thinking, "Surely there must be a reason why so many presenters have created so many slides with so much text information for decades!" I'll explain by giving the two big reasons I've discovered through talking with many presenters.

2.2 WHY TO AVOID TEXT-HEAVY SLIDES AND COMPLEXITY

2.2.1 Why presenters make text-heavy slides 1. *Fear of forgetting the story*

When asked why they put so much text in the slides, my clients first answer they are afraid they won't remember what to say. Therefore, they write out whole sentences in bullet point form.

There are some truly fundamental problems with writing the whole pitch on the slides.

1. *What you write is not what you speak*

When you write, you do so on the assumption that the words will be read. The content is designed for the rational brain to read through and process. It's more formal and detailed.

But when you begin to speak to an audience, you realise the spoken word is different from the written word, and you feel that difference immediately. You hear yourself speaking and start questioning yourself in your mind: "That doesn't sound right! Why did you say it like that? You would never normally speak this way!"

I'll give you an example. You might very well write in a document:

"We've developed a six-point plan based on the established pillars of the company's growth acceleration plan, and have put together a multi-faceted, multi-disciplinary team. We will execute the plan according to agreed targets, and in line with that strategy over the coming two quarters."

If you speak like this to an audience, people (at best) will think you're a bit boring, and at worst, completely nuts! Try reading that paragraph aloud to yourself, and you'll feel it.

What you might say in a pitch is:

"We've looked at where the company's growth is coming from and put together a plan that is focused on one part of it. Our targets are in place, we've got the right people and skills in the team, and over the next six months, we're going to make it happen!"

This is more direct language, less formal and matches what you might say to a friend over coffee.

The goal is to create a slide that is a platform for the point you want to make, for what you really want to say. Fully written sentences feel unnatural both to the presenter and to the audience.

2. *You can only read exactly what is written on the slide*

Have you ever been in a pitch or presentation where the speaker clicks to a new slide, jammed with content, and after a quick look at it says, "Well, I won't go through all these points because of time, so let me summarise..." Then they go ahead and say a whole load of stuff that is not on the slide. Infuriating, right?

The problem for the audience, is that they cannot read and listen at the same time.

I often hear: "We'll just leave these bullet points in for them to read, not for us to say." But the brain is not equipped to do both at the same time. It's simply impossible to hear a person present and read something different on the slide. Your attention goes to one or the other.

The only other option is for the presenter to read each bullet point, painfully, word for word. This approach results in robotic presenting, sending the audience's attention off into their mobile phones.

115

What's more, you can listen at 150 words per minute and read at 260 words per minute. This means that if you are presented with a slide of six bullet points with a total of around 100 words on the screen, in a heartbeat, your brain does a very intuitive calculation: "Which can I do faster? Listen to what the presenter has to say or read the text? Ah yes, reading is quicker." The audience goes off and reads for 20 to 25 seconds and then wonders, "Erm, what was he saying?"

Putting lots of words on the slide means you as the presenter must read everything aloud. And that's simply not effective in helping increase understanding. In fact, you *decrease* understanding by adding more text information.

Here's how to solve the problem of writing too much on slides.

Convert words into visuals and icons. Instead of filling the slides with text, choose the key words to help you remember the storyline and help the audience understand it. When you combine some key words with icons or images, it provides you the trigger you need to remember what you are about to tell.

Another approach is an image and a statement, either full screen with an overlay or half screen with clean text. It'll give you a reminder and a platform for the point you want to emphasise, and it helps the audience to keep track. I'll share more about how to do this in the coming pages.

Use slides as a quick reminder of what you want to say, as well as to help the audience know the theme of this section of the story.

116

2.2.2 Why presenters make text-heavy slides *2. They need to send the slides before or after the pitch*

The second answer my clients give when asked about the text-heavy slides, is "We need to send them for people to read."

Here's brutal reality about sending slides before or after: *95 percent of slide decks sent are never opened!*

People are incredibly busy and a 42-slide presentation jammed with text is not high on most people's list of priorities.

Naturally there are situations where it is either expected (e.g. the boss told you to do it!) or when there really is a high likeli-hood that it will be read (e.g. when an investor or the Board specifically requested it). Here's what to do when it's required.

Design two decks, one to present and one to send

The pitch deck that you present should be visual, with minimal words. It's supported by icons and images to emphasise what you say. As you are not there to *tell* the story, the pitch deck you send should contain more detail to explain the background information and context.

See below two examples of the same part of a story. The first to present, the second to send.

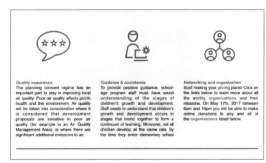

If you send the first type of slide, the reader will understand very little. However, this is great to present with because you can explain verbally the context with your insight, emphasis and passion.

If you present using the second slide, nobody will listen to you. They will just start reading! However, this slide is perfect to send afterwards because you are not there to give the background details. If someone is triggered by the face-to-face pitch and reads your deck with more details later, they get a reminder of your short pitch and more information to digest more carefully.

If this seems like more work... well, it is! And it's worth it because the goal is to ensure the audience understands the story and is triggered into action. Doing the work to create two slide decks is a valuable investment of your time.

2.2.3 Reducing complexity

All the tools so far focused on reducing complexity, increasing understanding for the audience and making it easier for the listeners to process the information.

There is a big reason why slides should be easier on the eye. When faced with complexity, we all naturally switch off.

Instead of taking time to work through the complex information – which may or may not be interesting or useful – you stop paying attention. Instinctively you feel the time may not be well-invested in trying to understand difficult details.

Your task as pitcher is to give signals to the audience there that this pitch will be easy to understand. One of the most effective ways is to reduce complexity on slides. That way, information appears easier to grasp and gains more attention.

How? Reduce text, use visuals and keep content to a minimum per individual slide. Never be afraid to spread information and use more slides with less complexity per slide.

2.2.4 How many slides should I use?

Between 1 and 150! Or rather, there is no right answer to this question.

In the past, there was a perception that showing many slides was a bad thing. This was because most presenters crammed too much information on one slide, and each one took at least a minute (and often four or five!) to present.

I have a vivid memory of sitting through a presentation which, according to the agenda, was due to last 30 minutes. The second slide came up with over 15 different pieces of information on it – clipart, bubbles, process flow, text at point size 10... As the presenter started explaining, I noticed some numbers in the bottom right corner of the slide, and it said: '2/77'. That meant we had another 75 slides to go and the presenter had spent two minutes only explaining this one! Needless to say, that presentation did not finish in half an hour...

It's not the number of slides that counts, it's what you do with them.

Recently I delivered my slide deck for a 30-minute keynote. The organisers replied with a nervous email, asking if I would be able to manage to finish within the given time slot, because there were 103 slides in the deck. I ensured them that each slide had no more than three pieces of information, and many were on screen for no more than 10 seconds. I finished in 28 minutes.

A benefit of having more slides is that each time you advance from one to the next, you reset the audience's attention. This is not a reason in itself to create more slides! But be assured that if you find you need two to three slides per minute, it's not a negative in terms of audience focus.

119

What matters is creating slides that support the important points of a story, not matching any popular theory of how many slides should be used per minute. Decide what needs to be emphasised, and create easy-to-understand visuals that keep information separate and clear, so that at any given time, the audience knows what to focus on.

2.3 **IMAGES, ICONS, LOGOS AND FONTS**

In this section you'll see examples of how to create more visually oriented slides, instead of bullet points and text.

2.3.1 How to use images to bring your story to life

Use a full-screen image with a statement overlaid. This way, the image supports your message. And the statement is the theme for some 20 to 30 seconds of your pitch.

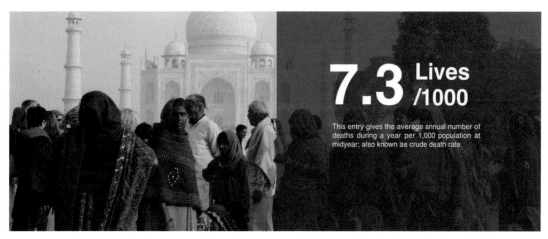

A way to create focus on the visual and the text is a half-screen image, together with a short and easy to read text.

You can use an image as a background texture for the key messages you want to tell in text.

122

When searching for images, think laterally. Look to use an image to express an idea, not just the specific words you want to say. (I will share some good sources for pictures later on.)

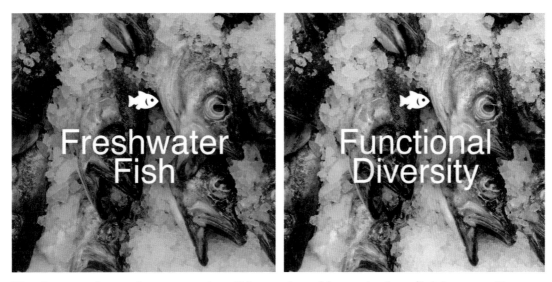

Use the same image in consecutive slides, and use blur and colour/brightness adjustments to show you've moved to a next step in the topic.

Use colourful and bright images that bring the story to life. Avoid dark and grey images, unless they match the idea you are bringing across.

If a person is in the image, have them face into the text – not away. This positioning directs the audience's attention to the key words.

124

If you want to show a screenshot, frame it in a laptop or phone, making it easier for the audience to understand instantly what they are looking at. Full-screen screenshots are confusing and look less professional.

2.3.2 **What to avoid when using images**

Ensure that your images have a high enough resolution to survive the latest screen technology. It might look fine on your laptop, but if there is a three-metre screen at the event you're presenting at, it might not look so great if it's only 300 x 200 pixels! Look for resolutions of at least 1920 x 1080 pixels. When in doubt, test the image on a larger screen.

Use a maximum of two key images. Using too many will draw focus away from the main message.

Avoid watermarked images. These previews from paid sites look very unprofessional.

Don't change the proportions dramatically. A stretched image looks strange and distracts the audience from the message.

Ensure that the text is easy to read if you use a background image. Make the image darker, reposition the text or change the font colour. Or choose a different image.

It's a deal!

128

Avoid fake stock photos with situations which are too perfect to be true!

Image sources: rights free
You can choose a completely safe approach by paying for pictures at places like Shutterstock, Getty Images and iStock. It's worth it for images you will use regularly, but can be expensive.

Note: If you plan to pick up images via a simple Google search, you'll most likely end up using a photo from one of these companies, which could cost you even more. You might think that the chances of getting sued are small. But webcrawlers and artificial intelligence are getting so effective that if you use a copyrighted picture, you have a high chance of getting found out. Getty and co. have serious lawyers who sue for thousands!

If you're looking for free pictures, check out the following resources which are growing fast at the time of going to press. They all offer completely rights-free images under Creative Commons licenses, which are available for commercial use.

Sites for
free images

That means you can use the pictures for any use at all, without attribution to the creators. (As a creator myself, I occasionally pay the optional fee for images that these sites sometimes ask for. Please do consider doing the same.)

- Pixabay.com
- Pexels.com
- Unsplash.com
- Sitebuilderreport.com/stock-up
- Freerangestock.com

You can also find a full list of recommended sites at pitchtowin.com/free-image-sites.

Finally, the easiest way to find photos exactly to your liking is to generate your own! Keep an eye out for moments that express part of your story. Customers using your product, pitchers on stage, visitors at the office, your favourite sports event... these can all be sources of great images for your pitch. Just make sure anyone who shows up in the picture agrees with appearing in your presentation.

ACTION

Action – 15-minute task – Turn text into visuals.

1. Review a recent pitch deck and check if there are any slides with too much text. If you don't have any – great, you're done! However, if you did find a few text-heavy slides, go on to step 2.
2. Replace the sentences with images, using the sources mentioned in this chapter. If still needed, keep a few key words or one headline sentence to remind you of the theme of the slide.
3. Ensure any important facts are large and highlighted: key metrics, awards, customer logos.

Try this for three to five slides to begin with and work on them until they look great. Once you've done this, it will be easier to apply the same approach to the whole slide deck.

2.3.3 Use icons for concepts

Icons are an easy way to express an idea quickly and simply, as they are very familiar. Audiences see icons in numerous apps they use every day, and they can shortcut a lot of explanation and text on a slide.

Icons transcend language barriers and are less likely to have love-hate reactions, which photos may create. For example, some members of the audience may simply dislike the look of a person or animal in a photograph, whereas icons are com-

pletely neutral and informational. Icons also have technical benefits. They work on all screen sizes, and create smaller files.

You may find it difficult to picture how to replace a slide with bullets and text, with icons. Yet a simple combination of an icon and a couple of keywords are enough for the audience to follow the story, and for you to remember where you are in the presentation. This is shown in these example slides:

130

Be sure to use .png-versions of the icons, with transparency in the background. That means that there won't be distracting white space around the icons, if they are placed on a coloured background.

Ideally, find icons from one source with one colour. This gives a consistency in style and feeling. You might need to recolour an icon to match the standard colours. Although that is not possible yet in Keynote, it's easy to do in PowerPoint, Photoshop and various other cheap and free image editing tools.

Icon sources: rights free
There are fewer sources for rights free Creative Commons icons, but a great place is thenounproject.com. They offer thousands of free icons and the yearly fee of $39,99 gets you access to their complete collection of over a million designs.

Another excellent source is fontawesome.com. This is a small but comprehensive collection of consistently styled icons that should cover your main pitch deck needs.

131

And finally, check out iconfinder.com and flaticon.com. Both have plenty of free icons and paid options that make searching and downloading easy.

Action – 15-minute task – Use icons to express concepts and highlight simple points.

1. Review a recent pitch deck and check if you can replace any words with icons.
2. Use the suggested sources to find icons that work for you. Keep a consistent style and colour of icons.

132

As with the exercise for using images, try turning text into icons for three to five slides to begin with and work on them until they look great. Once you've done this it will be easier to roll out the same approach to your complete slide deck.

2.3.4 Keep visuals in tune with your brand

For non-designers, the hardest thing to manage is consistency. Designers have an eye for this, they can instantly look over a slide deck, website or promo movie and point out inconsistencies.

For us non-designers, the task is to keep it simple. Maintain a similar style of images, minimise the variety of coloured backgrounds you use, keep font colours to black or white, with one accent colour, and continually ask yourself: "Does this image and colour match the style, tone and message of our company?"

Fonts are often where it goes wrong. Two for titles, another couple for subtitles, a few others for body text. It can look like an explosion in a type factory! The key is once again consistency. Choose only one headline font and one body text font. Ideally this matches the brand fonts for the website and other communication materials.

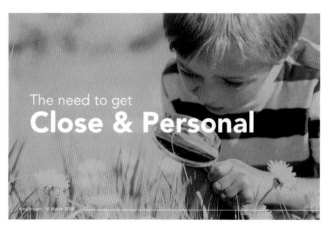

Choose fonts with a light and a bold option. This gives you the opportunity to create hierarchy, and put the focus on the most important points on the slide.

The safest source is Google Fonts. Their fonts work both online and offline and are completely free. When you arrive at a location where they don't have your font installed, it's easy to download the font and install it. You can immediately go ahead with your pitch.

2.3.5 How to use fonts to communicate your message

Every use of a font communicates more than the written words. You influence what people think, focus on and feel, because of your typography. The following slide examples give some ideas of how to create the impact you want, through the specific use of text and fonts.

133

Focus is created by...

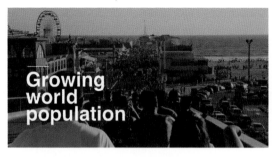 

....whether text is bold or not...

134

...whether it's large or small...

....and by colours to accent key words or ideas.

Treating

CLIENT

as a

FRIEND

The spacing between letters can give a different focus and feeling too.

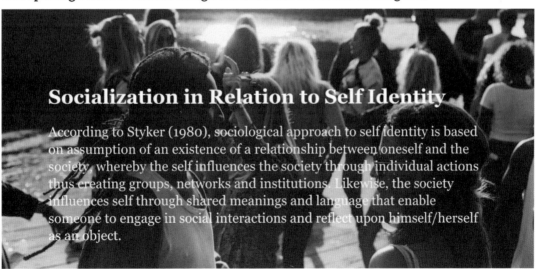

Socialization in Relation to Self Identity

According to Styker (1980), sociological approach to self identity is based on assumption of an existence of a relationship between oneself and the society, whereby the self influences the society through individual actions thus creating groups, networks and institutions. Likewise, the society influences self through shared meanings and language that enable someone to engage in social interactions and reflect upon himself/herself as an object.

And the most important point about text is **don't use too much!**

Keep the amount of information per slide to a minimum, and keep enough space in-between the pieces of text or key words. This approach allows the audience to receive the key messages more easily. They simply have to do less work to understand what you want to communicate.

136

2.4 HOW TO USE NUMBERS, ANIMATION AND VIDEO, AND AVOID ONE THING

2.4.1 Bite the bullet! Why bullet points don't work

Over the years, Microsoft developed numerous templates to make it easier for you to build slide presentations. Almost every single template is loaded with bullet points. And every time you hit 'New slide', a new list of bullets pops up, just waiting to be filled up with a load of text.

Bullet points were originally intended to help increase clarity by separating the content and ensuring it's clear that one piece of information is different from the next. In theory, this makes a slide easier to read and improves understanding.

This idea is only true for the second kind of slide deck I described, the presentation that is sent and *intended* to be read. For slides that will be presented, bullets have the completely opposite effect.

Bullet points give the audience an instant visual trigger: "This is a bullet-point type of pitch." Their brains quickly connect to all the associations they have with earlier bullet-point pitches. "What were all those pitches like? Awful! Time to tune out and find something useful to do… Where's my mobile phone?"

The two examples below show a way to separate information without bullet points. Reduce the text to a few key words and use space between the lines. Also cut down from five or six bullet points to a maximum of three statements per slide.

This way the audience's brains will not get overwhelmed by complexity. The story becomes easier to pay attention to and takes less time to absorb.

If you do need bullet points to separate information, there is probably too much information on the slide. Spread the information across more slides and the need for bullet points will disappear.

Challenge yourself to remove all bullet points from your next pitch. You might be surprised how easy it is to shake off those PowerPoint templates.

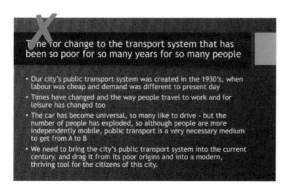

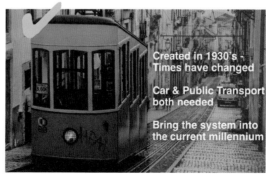

Action – 10 to 15-minute task – Remove all bullet points.

1. Review your slide deck and check for bullet points.
2. Replace the bullets with key words, images or icons.
3. If you have too much information and your slide is too crowded, spread the information over two or more slides.

138

2.4.2 How to present numbers: Keep data points to a maximum of three

You've already seen how the Power of Three helps to structure content in the storyline. You can also apply it to great effect when presenting data.

Have you ever seen a chart brought up on screen with numbers in a small font, lines and bars, and very small text showing in deep detail the source of the data?

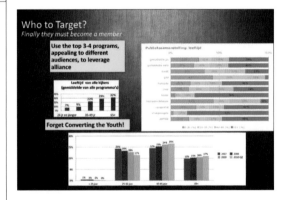

I've seen it so many times that I started asking why pitchers do it. They say:

"I want them to believe our explanation is based on real numbers."

"They need to know the data comes from a good source."

"I didn't want them to think I'd just made it up."

The problem is, a slide like this causes the listeners' brains to scream: *"Arrgghh! Complexity! Too much information! Run away!"* And their attention is gone.

I've also noticed that if you present more than three data points, the audience starts to analyse, and even worse, question the data. Up to three is often enough to convince, but more information means more to think about.

When your time is so precious you don't want your audience to think too much! Three numbers are enough on any one slide.

In a pitch there is no need to quote the source, unless it adds real credibility and you can do it in half a sentence. Pick the conclusions of the research you are

quoting or the market data you've found. You can explain the details in a follow-up discussion.

Here's an example of four data points. This slide is a modification of the pitch that successful Dutch startup SendCloud made at Startupbootcamp Demo Day. But this is not how they actually presented. The real slide comes later.

You'll see that the four pieces of data are well-designed. But the audience will start to analyse. "100K per month. And 100K packages? Does that mean each package costs €1? Oh, but that's the total packages, and they've been growing at six percent per month, so that means.." Their atten-

139

tion is lost on the analysis, instead of being focused on the point the pitcher wants to make.

Robin Dohmen, who was chief of design at Startupbootcamp at the time, made sure this didn't happen. He spread the data across two different slides.

Robin chose to make two slides because there were two separate points being made. The first: We have established ourselves and achieved penetration into the market.

140

The second: We are growing, from a strong base of monthly revenue.

By separating these two messages across two slides, the audience was guided on where to focus their attention.

One last thing about data. Don't be afraid to put the big numbers on the screen. If you have just reached 10,000 users, make it bold, verbally and visually.

10.000 users

Why does it matter? Because 10,000 is an important number and if someone in the audience drops their attention for just half a second, they may not hear it. By saying it and showing it nice and large on the screen, you show them this is a number that matters. And you increase the chance that they remember that number.

Presenting traction. The art of the customer logo

When showing your success so far, make sure the most important information jumps out. I've seen slides where startups or innovation teams mix up less-known logos with well-known brands, with the same size and priority given to, say, a partnership with Smith & Co. as to that with Samsung or IKEA.

142

Create a hierarchy of a maximum of three big brands and then cluster the others underneath. This approach gives two separate messages. Firstly, these three big brands believe in us and secondly, so do many others.

This positioning helps create clarity and ensures the audience doesn't miss an important customer or partnership.

ACTION

Action – 10-minute task – Present your traction with a hierarchy.

1. If you have sales or well-known customers, choose the three biggest.
2. Create a slide that matches the guidelines given in this chapter. Three large brands and logos, with other logos at a consistent size, nicely aligned, underneath.
3. You can also put the three best-known brands on one slide and make a second slide with the lesser-known customers or partnerships.

More information
on animations

2.4.3 Alignment: Put everything straight in your audience's minds

As humans, we like order. When we see objects out of line, we feel uneasy and want to set them straight. The same goes for slides, non-aligned elements distract us, while good alignment gives a subconscious feeling of comfort.

If you have a text and icon slide, it's comfortable to see the three elements nicely spaced and lined up, with the text left, right or centre aligned. If there are inconsistencies it looks sloppy and unprofessional.

Keep applying order and simplicity in everything your audience sees on the screen.

2.4.4 How animation can add value and take it away too!

Animation in slides has a very bad name, and for good reason.

In the '90s, PowerPoint introduced all kinds of possibilities for moving text and objects into and around the screen, causing presenters to experiment. The results were terrible! Text bouncing up and down, images flying in from left and right and revolving logos galore.

143

This doesn't mean animation is fundamentally bad. It simply means you should use it with care. Movement of objects and text with a purpose to emphasise, helps create focus.

Choose a small selection of animations: one or maximum two for text and one or two for images and icons.

If you have a series of elements to show on one slide because they are interconnected, build it up by animating one element at a time, to match what you are talking about.

144

Slide transitions (animation from one slide to the next) also help make clear to the audience that you are talking about something new. Once again, keep it simple. Select minimal transitions, such as fade to black, or dissolve.

There is a short movie to explain this further at pitchtowin.com/animation-for-good.

ACTION

Action – 10 minute task – Check the animations in your deck.
1. Go through your slides in presentation mode and check how the animation is adding or distracting.
2. Choose one standard animation for images and icons and one for all text. Apply it throughout the pitch deck.
3. Do the same with slide transitions. Choose one or two and apply to all slides (e.g. fade to black; dissolve).

2.4.5 **When and how to use video**
You can deliver a lot of information in a short time with video. Audiences generally enjoy watching movies, which can capture a bigger world than the confines of the room you're pitching in.

Use video for a demo of your product, a customer giving a product reference or an animated movie to show the vision of what your product can do. Check the chapter about Product Demo (on page 52) to review how this can work.

There are several pitfalls to avoid.

Don't make the video the first thing they see

If you are announced with a big fanfare: "And now, here's John to tell how he's changing the world of boat sharing!", and you come on and say: "Hi, let me show you a video first," you lose the momentum of the applause. It also takes the focus off you as the entrepreneur.

They've come to hear your story and the video supports that story, it is not the story itself. Ensure there are at least 30 seconds of you talking before the movie starts, so they can tune into you first.

Keep it short!

If you've got a three-minute pitch, no more than 20 to 25 seconds should be taken up by a movie. That's already 10 to 15 percent of the whole time available to pitch! People want to hear you, they

can watch a video at home. If the pitch is longer, I would advise an absolute maximum of 45 seconds for any movie you show.

Make sure the movie starts automatically

In PowerPoint, if you don't set the movie to play automatically, you need to click on the screen to make it play. If you use a clicker it will simply take you straight to the next slide without playing the video. (This problem doesn't exist in Keynote where movies play automatically and also when you click.)

Ensure you know the last thing you'll say before the movie starts, and remember that when you transition to the next slide, the movie will begin. This makes the video a more seamless part of the pitch and positions you as more professional.

Test, test and test again!

Later I'll talk about delivering your files. For now, note that movies can cause a lot of complication. Make sure in advance that the movie plays on the computer and screen that will be used for your pitch. Check that the sound works and that it plays for the length of time you expect. There's nothing worse than a technical hitch when you are under time pressure!

2.5 THE TECHNICAL STUFF

2.5.1 Slide software options

The question "Which software should I use?" is asked often. To begin with, my answer is: "Software is not important." Going through the process I've described to get the story straight is the most important aspect of creating good slides. It enables you to focus solely on visuals, with the storyline already in the bag.

Once you've developed a storyline that's clear and you feel sure of, the next step is choosing which tool you'll use to emphasise that story. There are some differences among the available software options that could affect that choice. Here are the big three:

PowerPoint

It's much abused, yet used around the world by 300 million people. Its biggest benefit is being universal, meaning you can send a PowerPoint presentation anywhere and almost certainly it will work well on someone else's computer. It has most of the functionality you could possibly need and it's pretty easy to use if you're familiar with Microsoft Office products. There are versions for both Windows and Mac which is a big plus.

Keynote

Apple's answer to PowerPoint works on almost the same principles. Within a couple of hours of getting used to the tools, especially if you've used PowerPoint before, you'll be able to use Keynote. It's also cheap.

Perhaps the biggest downside is that it's for Mac only. Even at major conferences, they can have problems with managing Keynote files, so check in advance if this will cause a problem at the location you're pitching.

146

Keynote benefits versus PowerPoint

There is some important functionality in Keynote that doesn't appear in Power-Point, making it a favourite for designers.

There are various attractive and effective animations in Keynote. Moving objects around the screen while editing is easier too. You can move pixel by pixel with the arrow keys and move 10 pixels at a time by holding the shift key. This is not available in PowerPoint.

Alignment is easier with automatic snap guides and integration with Apple media libraries (iTunes, Photos, etc.) makes finding and adding content easy.

If you want to lay a movie over something else, there is an opacity tool for video. As mentioned, starting movies automatically or after a timed delay is also possible. You can choose the thumbnail frame that the movie starts with, too. None of this is possible in PowerPoint.

You can open PowerPoint files in Keynote but PowerPoint won't open a Keynote file. Although you can export from Keynote to PowerPoint format, this often messes up animations and transitions, and can also cause text and font irregularities. Check, check and check again!

In conclusion, of these two giants Keynote is my recommendation, but PowerPoint is perfectly usable.

Prezi

There are a few alternatives to the Big Two, and a firm third place is held by Prezi. Formed as a startup in Hungary in 2009, they have gained some millions of users already.

If you are seeking to communicate complex issues and stories where various points are interrelated, Prezi can be very effective. You can zoom from an overview into close-up details effortlessly, and it gives you a big-picture view that is impossible with its bigger rivals.

147

The biggest downside is the toolset. It takes quite some time to learn how to use it, because the tools are very different from Apple or Microsoft. This generally results in only one person in the company or team being an expert. Then you must rely on one team member every time a change needs to be made.

There is also a tendency to create seasickness-inducing sways of zooming from one point to another, using the unique Prezi zoom feature for its own sake, rather than for a purpose.

148

If you're looking for an ambitious alternative, test it out and see if it works for you. However, if you are looking for a tool with a low-learning threshold, or for a bigger team, Prezi is not my recommendation.

What about Google Slides?

Slides is part of Google's suite of apps and while it's free, I find it almost useless. Google Docs is great for sharing your script and getting feedback from others, but Slides is pretty clunky and doesn't have all the needed features offered by other slide software. On top of that, you need to be online to use Google Slides, which is not always possible at every location. I'd strongly advise against using it.

2.5.2 **Pitchy: the magic alternative**
One new tool on the market is called Pitchy, which will save you 50 to 60 percent of time in developing your slides. You're guaranteed quality because the designers behind these tools are working on creating slides for pitchers like you, every day.

Pitchy is an online platform that guides you through the process of building your script, and based on the key words and meaning, generates options for design. It almost creates your slide deck for you automatically!

It works by analysing the script you write using artificial intelligence and by picking up on the meaning of what you want to communicate in each section of the pitch. It then serves up recommendations for images, icons and text, so that you can choose what suits your story best.

Get more information at mypitchy.com.

For full transparency: I am a cofounder of Pitchy.

2.5.3 Get the technical stuff right

Once you've decided on your software and have a well-prepared slide deck, you may need to deliver it to an organisation managing an event featuring a series of pitches. Here's what to check.

What format do they need?
The standard is now 16:9, but they might just need 4:3. If so, you'll need to remake your slides, so ask in advance to be sure. If you get this wrong, all your images will be squeezed and the text will end up in places you don't expect!

What software are they running?
If you're working with Keynote and they have PCs, you'll need to export to Power-Point, or ask if you can use your own computer. This last option works best, but sometimes it's just not possible.

Install the fonts
If they don't install the fonts, there is a chance your text will not look anything like it's supposed to. Send the fonts in advance and make sure to check that they have installed them.

When in doubt, use pdf!
The most secure way to be sure everything looks right, is to export everything to pdf as a backup. It's the most universal format and it can be used in full-screen mode for presentation. Once again Keynote wins, because it can export to pdf slide by slide, or with a new page per animation. That means you can simulate the animations when presenting using pdf. In PowerPoint each slide exports as a page and animations are lost.

149

2.5.4 The smartest way to deliver your presentation

This is so helpful that I want to credit my designer friend and business partner Robin Dohmen for this tip (he also helped create the slide examples in this book). He showed me an almost no-fail way to deliver presentations to colleagues, conferences and other locations where you'll present.

First create a folder called **1. Install These Fonts.** Place all relevant fonts in this folder.

Next create a folder called **2. Open This Presentation.** Place the presentation here.

Finally create a folder called **3. Check This PDF.** Place a pdf of the latest version of the presentation. The organisation can refer to it when checking to see if the installation went well.

After you've prepared the three folders, make a zip file of them, title the file with your name and the event, and send it with WeTransfer if the zip file is over 10MB.

I've done this many times in the last few years, and there has never been any confusion over which fonts are needed, or any incorrect installation. Brilliant!

150

2.5.5 And for the Big Ones... hire a designer!

You are now able to create strong, inspiring pitch decks that support your story, even if you're not a designer. Yet when you have a Big One coming up, I'd recommend hiring an expert.

Designers see things in a different manner. They can add polish and professionalism in a way that is difficult to quantify. Giving a TED Talk? Speaking in front of 200+ people? Got a once-in-a-lifetime opportunity with that big investor? Then put money into a designer. He or she will be able to create a pitch deck that you will use for a long time. You can learn from the work they do too, which will help you elevate your own slide design work.

My personal recommendation is of course Robin Dohmen. He and I have worked on numerous projects and pitch decks for startups and major corporates. You can contact him at robin@owow.io.

INTERVIEW PATRICK DE ZEEUW

Co-founder of Startup-bootcamp, Innoleaps and The Talent Institute.

Why is pitching important?
Almost all startups underestimate the importance of being able to explain in just a few minutes what you're doing, why it's relevant for the end-user and why you're so passionate about what you are doing.

If you're not able to tell this clearly, you'll miss out on many opportunities. Not only with possible customers, but also potential investors, potential employees and anybody who might be able to spread your message.

Passion is very important.Your audience needs to see the fire in your eyes because then the chances of them believing in your story and following up become bigger.

This all means that pitching is an essential element of doing business in general, not just raising investment. If you're not able to explain your story it will be very hard for people to buy or invest in your product.

Why does it matter to be able to get your message across in a short time?
Simple, people get distracted very easily! If you're not able to keep my attention while you explain to me in the first one or two minutes, probably I lose track. This is truer than ever with all the devices we have and all the messages we're getting. Attention spans are becoming shorter than ever.

What makes you sit up and take notice in a pitch? What's most likely to grab your attention?
A clear message, who's your customer and what you are solving. Relevant numbers, hardcore metrics because numbers always speak and convince. And the passion of the person pitching. Don't just touch me in the brain on the rational side,

it's also important to touch me in the heart on the non-rational side.

The story behind the whole thing matters too. Being able to explain *why* you're doing this counts because setting up and running a business is extremely hard. If you can explain why you decided to do this one thing and nothing else, why you want this problem solved, then that touches me personally. Maybe it's not the case for everyone. I'm a very passionate person so for me, it's a very important thing. If it's just a rational story, I'm less likely to buy into it, even if it's a great opportunity.

If you had to choose one thing to be good in a pitch – content, or delivery – which would you choose?
Content! Delivery is of course incredibly important, because if you can't bring that message across then the content won't shine. But if the delivery is great and the content is really poor or not credible, I'm not going to believe you! And I might be able to see past a badly delivered pitch with great content.

The skills of pitching can be learned but if your proposition isn't thought through, your team is not that strong, or you cannot explain what problem you're solving for whom, then it's never going to fly. Content and hard facts matter and pitchers can be helped with training to bring that story across better.

Does pitching matter in a big company? Don't they just want to know the numbers and ROI?
I experience that pitching matters there too, because you find there are more and more internal innovation projects in large corporates. The kinds of people who make the decisions about you getting the resources, time or people, are more or less similar to the investors a startup needs to convince. If you can't bring that message across to the CEO, CFO or your boss, then you will miss out on opportunities.

This has become way more important in large corporates than it was six or seven years ago, because there is so much more activity on the innovation side. Major

153

companies know they need to innovate furiously, develop new business models, use available technology to be able to grow. That means they need to fill up their funnel with MVPs (Minimum Viable Products). They also need more internal founders and finding the right talent for that task is really difficult.

The danger is that they choose the idea first and not focus on the right people to execute, which is what we do with startups at Startupbootcamp and Innoleaps, we focus on the team first. You need those very driven, very passionate people to bring the message of new opportunities across internally. That's where pitching becomes really important.

Does having professional slides influence the quality of the pitch?
I think it's extremely important, especially if you have the wrong slides! A lot of text and bullet points dilute the message. The power of the pitch is increased by having the right visuals and the slides should always strengthen the storyline. It shouldn't tell the story, but rather enhance it with another sense in play.

You can use humour in visuals, drama, you can do all kinds of things to grab the attention of the audience. We've learned that less text and stronger graphics and images can lift a pitch from an 8 to a 9. The opposite is also true. If you have really ugly visuals, it says something about your company. If your slides are badly designed, you miss an opportunity to make a good impression! If your slides have a strong layout and powerful visuals, you have a strong message and you show that you take things seriously. This can only make the impression you want to make stronger and it tells something about your attitude as a company. It's a huge missed chance if you don't invest in the design of your presentation. ●

DELIVER.

THREE

3.1 <u>NON-VERBAL COMMUNICATION</u>

You have a storyline and script that will get your message understood, makes the audience remember the big issues and feel the professionalism of your approach.

You also have a set of visuals that support the story and emphasise the most important points. Now it's time to work on the final piece of the puzzle: delivery!

How are you going to tell this story in a way that creates buy-in, that conveys the emotion you want to, and – most of all – suits you as a person?

3.1.1 How to keep audience attention and reset it

It's a shocking statistic that the human attention span has reduced by over 50 percent in the last 15 years. Why? Because of the way we consume information every day.

Twenty years ago, we would sit and read a book. We weren't invited every nine seconds to read another book, buy something, check what our friends or work contacts are up to at that particular moment. Yet that is how we read today.

Websites, blogs and even books are constantly and actively interrupted by all manner of offers to do something different. (As I am writing this, I receive a notification that someone liked my recent LinkedIn blog post. Better check who that was... No! Back to the book!)

I've experimented with attention spans. For example, I once showed a group of twenty people one of the most interesting TED Talks ever. I told them it was five minutes long and after just two and a half minutes, a collective restlessness rippled through the audience. No matter how interesting the content, we cannot pay attention to one thing for minutes on end.

Let's also not forget the human reality. While giving your pitch is the most important thing in your life at that moment (as it should be!), it simply isn't the same for the audience.

Investors see hundreds of pitches per year, and so do Board members. They are human beings, with bosses, colleagues, kids and husbands, wives and partners. They have a roof that needs fixing, a bill that needs paying or a lawyer that's telling them: "You're in trouble!" And anything else that happens in daily life, that might cause their attention to drift off into the distance...

158

Audiences need their attention to be spiked and reset regularly with something new, surprising, exciting or impressive. Their attention is like a butterfly, flitting between your pitch and all the other stuff in their head, their phone or wearable. It's up to you to keep them focused on your story.

Along the way of your pitch, you need to feed the audience with new information, ideally every 30 seconds. Long explanations of product and technology just don't work. Give them short, sharp statements of the value you bring, along with a clear structure, a strong opening, the Power of Three to keep it simple, and a strong closing. These are all effective in keeping attention.

Here is a selection of more tools that will help raise your audience's focus, and convince them that you are a true professional.

3.1.2 Movement

Using movement means making conscious decisions about taking a variety of positions in the room or on stage, and stepping from one position to another. (We'll talk about hand movements and gestures later.)

You may have seen 'pacers', presenters who can't stop walking left and right, and back again. This causes a lot of distraction for the audience and makes it very difficult to concentrate. Rocking backwards and forwards, or constantly shifting weight from foot to foot, are other presenter habits that take the audience's attention away from the point of their talk. These kinds of movement do nothing to help the audience.

In order for your movement to help signify something like a change of subject, a transition, a journey from the past to the future, you need to choose two to three positions on the stage or in the room, and make conscious decisions about when you will move from one position to the other.

I say *conscious* decisions, because if you don't decide in advance, movement might happen by accident. When you are nervous or just full of energy, you might end up constantly on the move.

When you get to the end of a certain phase of the pitch, you could say: "Okay, that's the problem our customers are facing, so how do we solve it?" And as you say this sentence, move from one position to the other. When you get to the new position, explain your solution while standing solidly in one place.

Take a look at how Steve Jobs used movement in his iPhone launches. He didn't walk across the room when he said: "Apple reinvents the phone." He faced his audience – legs slightly apart, feet firmly on the ground – and looked straight at them. Jobs wanted to make a *statement,* telling: "This is how it is." At moments of truth like these, it's best to be grounded and still, fully engaged with the audience.

In contrast, when Jobs said things like: "The designers and I were wondering, how will we tackle this?", he might have walked across the stage, almost in a thinking pose. This was a signal to tell you: "We were trying to get ourselves to think in a new way, to get ourselves from A, to B."

When he resolved that question, by saying: "Our conclusion was this," he took a firm, grounded position again and made his statement.

Think about where a change of position will help you move the story along.

But moving isn't always an option. Be sure that you have the possibility to walk from A to B, as there may be some restrictions in the location you're presenting at. For example, if there is specific lighting on stage you might need to remain with-in a certain area to stay in the light. If you are pitching in a small room, remaining in one position is probably the best choice.

No matter where and what you pitch, I recommend being 'grounded' at the opening and closing seconds of your pitch. The opening is a moment for the

160

Action – 20 to 30-minute task – Check your emphasising movement options.

1. Look at the area where you will present, a stage or a room. Is there an opportunity to move or do you need to stay in one place?

2. Review your pitch and note any moments of transition. Learnings, thinking, journeys or moments where the pitch really changes gear in focus. Obvious changes are from problem to solution, or finishing the investment request and moving on to the team.

3. Try doing a run-through of the pitch, focusing on your movement from one place to another at the times you've chosen. Does it feel natural? Do you feel these movements add to the energy of the pitch?

4. Film yourself doing the run-through and review it from the point of view of an audience member. Do the chosen movements help increase understanding?

5. Review the film, adjust and do a run-through on film at least three times, so you get used to the new way of presenting. Start to feel whether the movements suit you and the pitch, or whether you are better to take one position and stick to it.

audience to tune in to you, with minimum distraction. And the closing is the wrap-up with statements you want them to remember.

3.1.3 Eyes: Share the contact, share the love

Have you ever had the experience where you're in a meeting, and the presenter focuses his attention on you, excluding the other people listening? Or she only talks to one or two people in the room, excluding you? This focus makes everyone feel very uncomfortable. Regardless of the size of the audience, make a connection with everyone through eye contact.

One piece of advice I often have to shake out of clients is this: "Look at a point above the audience, at the back of the room. Don't try to make eye contact with the audience." If you hear this advice, please ignore it!

Just try the following. Ask a friend to explain what he or she had for dinner yesterday, without making eye contact with you. Your friend is not allowed to look you in the eyes and you can't try to make eye contact either.

Weird, isn't it? You feel strange, your friend feels awkward, and no-one is happy! It's totally unnatural. Most cultures highly value eye contact and expect it. When a person doesn't connect with their eyes, you're left with a feeling of distrust, worry or insecurity.

Share your eye contact evenly. Shift it every few seconds, as smoothly as possible. Look for a break in a sentence or the end of one, to make the transition from one person or one part of the room to another. This gives a natural feeling for the audience and helps you connect with everyone.

Here's how you manage eye contact with a variety of sizes of audience.

Small: 1 to 10 people around a table

Ensure you involve everyone, as evenly as possible. One tendency is that if there are,

161

for example, five people on one side of the table and two on the other, those two can be forgotten. Make a conscious choice to include everyone.

Medium: 10 to 50 people
In this case you can still make eye contact on an individual basis with a large part of the audience. Especially look out for familiar faces who support you. Catching their eye will give you energy and positivity.

Large: 50+ people
As soon as the audience gets a little larger, it becomes harder to connect with individuals. Sometimes you can't even see the audience because of strong lighting.

Here's a tip I received from Tara Phillips, a highly experienced speech coach who has trained over 50 TEDx speakers as well as numerous executives from some of the largest companies.

"When you have a large audience spread out in front of you, make eye contact by scanning the audience in a letter W. Start at the far left, scan down to the near left, then scan over to the back centre of the audience, then near right, and finally far right." I've tested this out myself, and it works perfectly. (Thanks, Tara!)

Cultural note: In some regions, especially Asia, things can be different. Making little eye contact is not necessarily a sign of distrust or discomfort. In fact, it's rather an attempt to be less confronting, or even a sign of respect. If you are presenting to an Asian audience, keep eye contact with the group. However, don't be surprised if there is less eye contact in return.

3.1.4 Hands: Tell it like you're having coffee with a friend

One of the most common questions I get asked about body language is: "What do I do with my hands?"

Michael Diederich from Amsterdam's improvisation comedy house Boom Chicago explains: "When you go to the baker and you want two loaves of bread from differ-

162

Examples of
body language

ent parts of the bakery, what do you do? Without thinking, you gesture and point to the loaves you want to buy. In this situation, you don't think about what you might do with our hands, you just do it! Yet for some reason, when presenting in front of an audience this natural ability to gesture in line with your meaning gets lost."

The same goes if you are having a coffee with a friend. Subconsciously you use your hands to emphasise the words, emotions and facts that you believe are important. Ideally you do so in a pitch too.

You also need a place to rest your hands when you're not emphasising something. This can be simply touching your thumbs and index fingers loosely in front of you.

Just like with body movement, making conscious decisions matters. If you don't decide what you'll do with your hands or pay attention to it while practicing, you might end up putting a hand in a pocket

or a hand on a hip, or behind your back, and not even realise you're doing it.

The best way to discover this is to film yourself while practicing. Review the movie as an audience member and focus on your hand movements only. Are they adding to the understanding by emphasising facts or emotions? Or are your gestures distracting and unrelated to what you're saying?

If you're not sure, get someone else to give you very specific feedback on this aspect. Ask them to watch you pitch and focus on your hand movements. Based on your own observations and the feedback you receive, do another run-through while filming and focus on making the changes you choose.

Here are a few do's and don'ts to help find an effective way to use your hands.

3.1.5 Don'ts for hand gestures, what to avoid

Hands behind your back. This suggests you have something to hide or indicates an additional formality to the situation.

Hands in your pockets. It gives the signal: "I am casual about this subject." If that is your intention (and on some rare occasions, it might be), then it's fine to do so. However in most cases it reduces your professional image.

164

One way of avoiding this, is to empty your pockets before the talk. If you have some change, keys or a travel card in your pocket, they act as a magnet for your hands! It doesn't look good if you subconsciously jingle the change or keys with your hand while talking.

Hands on hips. This gives a message to the audience that you want to dominate them. There may be a few instances where this is your intention, but if you want to send a different message, avoid the hands-on-hips pose. Also, it's often interpreted as arrogance.

One arm gripping the other. You might see a presenter halfway through a pitch with one arm straight down and the other crossed directly over the body, grasping the straight arm. This is something we do for comfort when under stress, and the audience may interpret it as nervousness.

Gripping your hands tightly. Another signal of stress. As mentioned, when at rest, look to touch the thumb of one hand gently against one or two fingers of the other, as relaxed as you can.

Pointing is very confronting. There is a story that Bill Clinton in his early days pointed frequently during his speeches, and he consistently received terrible ratings. When he was advised to wrap his index finger below his thumb, it instantly changed his approval ratings. It's better to use open palms and a curved hand to emphasise, rather than point, unless you consciously want to give a confrontational message.

Making hand gestures for every syllable. This conveys a lack of importance. It seems like you are making a point for every single word. As a result, it reduces clarity of what the audience should focus on.

I know this to be a problem because I have a tendency to do it myself! Some years ago, I had coached two different pitchers to stop making continual gestures. I did so by showing them a film of their run-through, to demonstrate how it caused a hectic atmosphere around their pitches. A couple of months later, I entered a pitch competition for a startup I was working for at the time. I watched the video afterwards, and although we won, to my astonishment I found I was doing exactly the same as I had coached my clients *not* to do.

Filming yourself is the only way to find out what you do subconsciously that may distract your audience when you intend to add focus.

And last but not least... **Avoid the 'Tony Blair'.** You may be familiar with the former Prime Minister of Britain, who regularly joined the tips of all fingers of both hands. Every time I saw him do this, I wondered: "Why is he lying to me?"

It's a typical politician's gesture and since we have almost all stopped having blind faith in politicians, it's probably best to avoid copying noticeable aspects of their body language. Especially this hand gesture!

3.1.6 Do's for hand gestures

Call out the numbers physically. If you are listing several options or a number of qualities of your product, call out the number with your hands.

If there are three things to tell, first hold up three fingers as you say: "There are three things I want you to remember."

Next, hold one finger up for the first item, add a second finger for the next, and when you come to the last item, add a third finger.

This gives a stronger signal to the audience that these are the important items they need to remember and creates more attention and retention.

Separate parties into locations. If you are talking about partners and end users, position each one with a gesture in different locations. 'First you have our partners *(gesture with both hands to the right)*, and then you have our end users *(gesture with both hands to the left.)*' Each time you talk about either of these groups, gesture towards the place you positioned them. By doing this consistently, it helps the audience understand who you are talking about at any one time.

Create contrast, then bring together. If you want to say: "On the one hand there is this, and on the other hand, there is that...", don't just say it, but do it with your hands too. Equally, if two contrasting ideas can be brought together, then do that with your hands as well.

For example: "Usually customers have to choose between strong data security on the one hand *(gesture with your hands to the right)* and on the other hand smooth user experience with no friction *(gesture with your hands to the left.)* With our solution, customers don't have to choose – we offer both" *(gesture your left and right hand apart, then bring your hands together).*

Transition from audience left to right When you want to express a journey, you often show the transition by a physical movement from one place to another.

A strong way of communicating such ideas – from the past to the future, from the bad to the good, or from the old to the new – is to *be* that transition. Moving your hands from one place to another or even positioning yourself in two places to show the two different situations, can help the audience to understand it.

166

However, a common error is to make this physical change from the presenter's point of view, and not the audience's point of view.

In the western world, we read from left to right. That means we intuitively expect things to develop in that direction. When the presenter shows a development from his own perspective, it appears to the audience as a development from right to left, which is counter-intuitive.

Ensure you show these changes from the audience's perspective. It may be difficult for you at first, because it is opposite to what feels natural, but it will increase the comfort level of your audience. And that's all that matters.

Cultural note: If you are presenting to people who read from right to left (the Arabic and Jewish worlds and parts of Asia), show them transitions accordingly. It's all about the audience and thinking through what will feel most natural for them.

Action – 20 to 30-minute task – Have a look at your hands.

1. Do a run-through and film it, focusing solely on your hand gestures.
2. Review the film and make notes on:
   • When you emphasise things effectively;
   • When your hand movements detract from the story.
3. Do a new run-through focusing on changing only one of those distractions or adding one emphasis gesture.
4. Do this a few times, and you'll find making the new gestures starts to feel natural and you'll remember to remove the distractions.

3.1.7 Be present with legs and feet

Once a client told me: "David, I don't need help with stage presence. I'm a musician, I've been on stage a thousand times, just help me with the script and the rest will be fine."

I took him at his word and a few days later, in front of 50 people at an Investor Sneak Preview, he gave a four-minute pitch. From the first second to the last, he rocked backwards and forwards from his right foot in front, to his left foot behind. It was totally distracting and gave the impression he was nervous, while in reality he was the most confident person in the room.

Afterwards, I asked if he knew he had been doing this and he said: "I don't believe you." I showed him a film of the first minute of his pitch and he was shocked. He had no idea of this movements, it just happened.

When you're nervous, anxious or simply excited, your body can reveal these feelings. One of the most common ways is with legs and feet.

As I mentioned, constant movement signals the pitcher's anxiety. Crossed legs, feet at angles and weight heavily on one leg while leaning over to one side are all signs that the presenter is trying to comfort himself at a moment of stress.

Having your feet too close together gives the impression of not wanting to take up space. Too much space will make your stance look awkward and unnatural.

Be present and straight with no boundaries. Especially at the beginning, be 'grounded': Both feet firmly on the floor, a little space between your feet and square-on to the majority of the audience.

Make conscious decisions about how you stand and film yourself during a real pitch. This way you can see whether you communicate the message you truly want to express with the way you stand.

3.2 TIPS FOR PERSUASIVE SPEAKING

3.2.1 How to cut out fill words: One simple tool

In one training session, I asked a client to give a three-minute pitch. After 20 seconds, I realised he had a fill word and started noting every time he said it. At the end of the three minutes, I said to him: "Did you know you said 'Heh' 31 times during that pitch?" He replied, stunned: "I had no idea I said it even once!"

It's not uncommon to have at least one regularly repeated fill word. A word or short phrase that occupies space while you think. You say them out loud, because you feel awkward with silence. Under pressure in a meeting or on stage, you fill up the silence with a selection of more fill words and sounds.

The most common are: *Um, er, well, so, actually, next, but, in fact, you know, kind of, like...*

And my own personal favourite: OBVI-OUSLY. In my head, when someone says: "Obviously the problem causes stress," I ask the question: "If it's obvious, why are you telling me this?"

The solution is not to take fill words out completely. As human beings, we all 'um' and 'er' at times. Nonetheless, if they are noticeable to the audience, which happens when they are repeated too often in too short a space of time, it can become a serious distraction.

There is a tool that will help you massively reduce the use of fill words. It's called: *Taking a Moment*.

For example, if you are at an event with a series of pitches, you'll probably be introduced. As the audience is clapping, walk onto the stage and find your spot to start the pitch. Once you have taken your position, make sure you wait until the clapping is finished, take half a second to look at your audience, and start.

169

170

Taking a Moment gives a signal to the audience that you are in control and gives your brain time to connect with the first sentence. If you start speaking while you are moving into position, you feel you are in a hurry and that will show itself in the chaotic way in which you start talking.

Taking a Moment also applies when you are in a meeting and presenting your idea. Often there is a social opening, with coffee-pouring and quick introductions. Ensure that when the chit-chat is almost finished, you take control and announce firmly: "Okay, let's start!" Allow everyone to find their seats and when everyone is ready, give yourself a further half second, and start.

I've done experiments with these approaches and I have discovered that they reduce the number of fill words by between 50 to 90 percent.

So why does it work? I believe it gives the brain a signal that says: "Silence is okay!" Plus, that simple half second is enough to allow your brain to engage with the content and stay ahead of the talk. The pressure to fill silence is reduced and the distracting fill words evaporate.

3.2.2 Speak as a leader: The power of silence

One of the most noticeable qualities of charismatic speakers is their ability to pause and allow their audience to absorb the point they have just made. Silence is a truly powerful tool.

We have a tendency to cram as much information about our product and business into the limited time we have available. When faced with the confines of a three-minute pitch, most teams are struggling to finish on time.

Humans can't listen to too much information in too short a time, they need some time to process the input. That's why silence helps, we get enough time to think about what we've heard and remember it if we feel it is important.

One of the simplest ways to allow yourself the space for silence, is to reduce content. As I mentioned earlier, humans are able to listen and make sense of a maximum 150 words per minute. Therefore, target your script to around 130 to 140 words per minute. This will give enough speed to inject some energy, yet leave enough time for you to pause and allow room for the audience to absorb your biggest statements.

To check if you are doing this well, record yourself in a real pitch situation. Listen if there are pauses at the right moments and try to imagine yourself as an audience member. Is the pitch too fast? Can you follow the details? Do you get rest for the most important points to settle?

You can also get feedback by asking a team member or friend to listen and concentrate specifically on your speed and pauses. If you finally conclude that you are going too fast and don't give enough air around the key sentences, do some recorded run-throughs. Focus solely on

slowing down and pausing. Try doing it even uncomfortably slow and ask someone else how it sounds. It might be that you'll hit exactly the speed you should pitch at!

3.2.3 Avoid the curse of monotone

When you're under stress, you tend to forget to put emotion and expression into the words. Sometimes you hear a pitcher racing through so that they finish their story as quickly as possible. The worst result is monotone. A droning pitch with no vocal variation. It makes it hard for the listener to keep focused and nearly impossible to identify what is important in the story.

There are three ways to add variation to your vocals: Speed, Pitch and Volume.

Speed: Sometimes you need to talk a little faster to express excitement, but not too fast. Remember the 150 word per minute guideline! Slowing down can give a clear signal to the audience that this is a moment to listen carefully.

Pitch: Speaking with a higher voice indicates excitement or energy and speaking with a lower voice suggests something more serious.

Volume: You may think that key points need volume to indicate importance, yet speaking a little quieter can draw the audience in and cause the audience to listen more carefully.

There is no exact right and wrong in these three dimensions. What matters is variation and emphasising the right words. It can really change the meaning.

Sheila Schenkel, the co-author of one of my previous books, came up with a great sentence where putting focus on a different word each time, changes the meaning of the sentence, even though the words remain the same.

Anthony said that his boss did not commit a fraudulent act. It's a neutral statement.

*Anthony **said** that his boss did not commit a fraudulent act.* But we all know better.

*Anthony said that **his** boss did not commit a fraudulent act.* It was someone else's boss.

*Anthony said that his boss did **not** commit a fraudulent act.* His boss didn't do it!

*Anthony said that his boss did not commit a **fraudulent** act.* But he was definitely on the edge of legal!

You put emphasis on key words very naturally when talking to a friend over coffee. Ideally you do the same in a pitch.

Finally, the best way of all to overcome monotone and put real meaning into the words, is to be certain, honest and passionate about what you are trying to achieve. Keep connected to the content and ensure you believe and stand by every word you say.

172

You can view full pitches here

3.2.4 Where are YOU in this story? Get reconnected with the content

One of the biggest challenges as an entrepreneur or intrapreneur is that you pitch regularly. After telling the same story many times, it's easy to lose your energy and passion for the pitch.

Clarifying to your audience why you are driven to make this business happen, and why you believe this matters, is one of the most compelling ways to grab the audience's attention.

Take a look back at the Why you? section of the Pitch Canvas©, on page 72. You'll remember we covered how to identify your personal motivation for working on this problem.

We all love a story and we all love the ones about the hero overcoming the odds, the lead character battling on behalf of the underdog. Or simply an entrepreneur following her passion!

Make sure *you* are in the story both as part of the story and by being present and committed to the pitch you are giving.

173

Action – 20 to 30-minute task – Find the meaning and focus your energy.

1. Print your script and go through each sentence. Look for the two to three words that change the meaning of the sentence and underline them.
2. Do a run-through where you read from the script, putting more emphasis and energy on the key words. This will help you make clear what you tell and make it more understandable and memorable.

The best way to ensure that you remain fresh and energetic, is to keep connected with the big moments in your story. Remember how you felt when you signed the first customer? When you broke through and made a great new feature work? Remember when you landed your first big contract or someone simply emailed you to say how great your product is?

Those moments are the ones you live for! Connecting back to those moments in your pitch will ensure you keep some emotional connection to the story you are telling. Even if it's for the two hundredth time!

Here is a personal example: When I open my workshops, I explain how people listen more to those who can present well, and less to those who can't. To bring this home to the audience, I ask:

"Have you ever pitched an idea, and nobody listened? I've had that feeling myself. It burns you inside! You get home with fury and frustration bubbling every-

where. I don't want anyone to have that feeling."

I have told this story over 500 times to various audiences and to keep it fresh I connect to a time when I wasn't listened to. It was such a raw feeling that every time I tell it, I cannot help but feel emotional and become animated. Because it's something I genuinely care about, for me and for others.

Make that emotional connection to those big moments in your company's development, and you will find you will stay close to your story. It will also connect you even more closely to your audience.

If you try to solve more than one problem at a time, it will be more difficult to focus and truly solve the distracting elements that you've identified. You don't have to jump to perfection in one step. Simply take one step at a time and focus on continually improving your pitches.

174

3.2.5 Remove voice and body language distractions from your delivery

I can't emphasise enough that the best way to assess your body language, is to film yourself in a real stressful situation. Of course, no-one likes doing this! Watching yourself pitch is like watching the dentist do his work. Yet seeing yourself as your audience sees you, is essential. Only then can you assess how your body language and voice add to the meaning or increase distraction.

Action – 20 to 30-minute task – Film yourself and look out for voice and body language distractions.

1. Watch a movie of yourself pitching, and review the film as objectively as you can. Are there any repetitive movements that distract attention? Are you standing in a certain way, moving too much, waving your hands, or crossing your legs? Is there a word that you keep repeating? Are you simply speaking too quickly?

2. Each time you find something that needs to be changed, focus on that one thing. For example: If you find something repetitive and distracting in your hand gestures, focus solely on improving that one aspect. Turn that distracting gesture into something that creates emphasises, or turn it into a pause.

3. Repeat the first two steps until you're happy with how your body language and vocal use support your story to the fullest.

If you try to solve more than one problem at a time, it will be more difficult to focus and truly solve the distracting elements that you've identified. You don't have to jump to perfection in one step. Simply take one step at a time and focus on continually improving your pitches.

Filming yourself, reviewing, and taking your time to remove those distractions will pay you back massively. And you'll find yourself getting more confident that you are telling the story you really want to tell.

INTERVIEW ASTRID SONNEVELD

Founder of The Good-Shipping Program

You won the TEDx Amsterdam Award with your four-minute pitch. How did you enjoy the experience?
It was great. Such an amazingly warm and engaged audience! I had given several pitches before TEDx Amsterdam but never at a venue with as big a capacity as the Grand Hall of the Stadsschouwburg.

What was the most daunting part of pitching at TEDx Amsterdam?
The pitch was filmed and is made available on YouTube for many years to come. It's a moment when you know you can't make an error, so the pressure is on! But in the end, I enjoyed it, after some good preparation.

Do you think pitching a social enterprise is different to pitching a typical tech startup?
Yes, I think it is slightly different. You have to focus more on feelings, beliefs and values in your pitch. Without money as the primary driver to build your business, there is the need to address the importance and urgency of your effort. You need to explain why your idea is ripe to succeed right here and now, and that you are ready to make change happen and maintain the momentum.

What do you prefer, pitching to a small group of people, or a big audience? What's the difference?
Prior to TEDx, I thought I would prefer pitching to smaller rather than bigger audiences. Afterwards, I realised it is not so much about the size of the audience, but rather about the receptiveness of that audience. The biggest difference is the sense of intimacy. Not being able to make eye contact with a group of hundreds makes it more difficult truly to engage.

You have some great companies as part of The GoodShipping Program, such as Tony's Chocolonely, the popular Dutch chocolate company that aims to make their products free of slavery. How did you pitch them to join?

In a similar way as I did the pitch at TEDx but with some small adjustments. With Tony's, it was not so much about creating the sense of urgency, since it is the kind of company that invented the attitude of picking up the glove, doing what you should be doing and live up to your beliefs. Instead we focused more on the what-if scenario and the associated impact on society.

What's your best advice to anyone who is preparing for a pitch?

Know your audience and adjust the mix of your pitch ingredients accordingly. Oh, and smile! It will boost your self-confidence and feels like a firm connection with the audience. ●

You can see Astrid's pitch in the collection of full-length pitches at https://pitchtowin. com/book-pitch-examples3/#fullpitches

HOW TO MANAGE YOUR NERVES

4.1 ALL ABOUT NERVES

You are now at the point where you've got a great story, clear slides to support it and a practiced and confident delivery style. You are ready to go!

And yet... despite all this work, some of you may be blocked by one simple thing. Nerves.

**It's time to keep calm...
and pitch.**

4.1.1 A universal problem and tools to solve it

Imagine that you're waiting to make your pitch. Heart beating fast. Temperature rising. You're beginning to sweat. Pitching before an audience is something that makes you REALLY scared!

You start your pitch and can hardly think or breathe. You say something wrong and that inner voice starts yelling at you: *"Why did you say THAT?"* You say more things you don't want to say and do more things you don't want to do. It's starting to go horribly wrong...

If you've experienced this yourself, you are not alone. I've asked thousands of people the same question: "Do you get nervous when pitching or preparing to pitch?" It doesn't matter whether they are experienced professionals, young start-up founders, corporate leaders or young product managers. Over 90 percent confirm that pitching makes them very nervous.

There are several practical steps that can help you take control. The first is to do the work! Great preparation is the best way to reduce any anxiety and using the tools I've described in this book to Script, Design and Deliver your pitch will help you gain confidence.

Nevertheless, some people are still blocked with nerves and need help. So here is a set of tried and tested tools that will help you turn your nerves into energy. With these tools you can truly shine when it matters. They are fully tested and proven to solve over 90 percent of nerve problems for over 90 percent of people.

The first step is to understand why those nerves appear in the first place.

4.1.2 Why do you get nervous?

When you stand in front of an audience you experience a primeval, caveman response. You are one and they are many, and in the early ages of man this meant you would be eaten or beaten. The way you survived was to develop a fight or flight response. When you realised you were under attack, the body prepared you for both possibilities.

Two major reactions occur in the body when fight or flight kicks in. First, you get a big boost of adrenaline which prepares your muscles to act and increases your body temperature. This is why you often feel tense and start to sweat in the first seconds of a pitch.

Secondly, a part of your rational brain disconnects. You're not supposed to think when under attack, just do something! Hit, run, take action and don't waste any time doing so.

As a result of your brain partly disconnecting, there is a big chance of saying and doing things you don't want to say and do, if you haven't decided exactly what you are going to say in those first stressful seconds. There's an even bigger chance of forgetting the essentials you thought you could never forget.

I've researched and tested all kinds of approaches that help presenters deal with this stress. What follows are practical steps that have helped thousands of my clients to manage their nerves and turn them into energy. You can do the same things to take control too!

4.2 TIPS TO BEAT THE NERVES

4.2.1 The 60-second nerve buster

This single tip works for most people I've coached, and it's worked for me too. It's all about learning the first 60 seconds of your pitch.

The moments when you first stand up and begin to speak are the most stressful of all. That's when the fight or flight mechanism truly kicks in, because of that instinctive feeling that we are under attack.

I've interviewed many presenters about what it felt like in the first minute of their pitch, and they all gave similar replies:

"It was like an out-of-body experience…"

"I said things I absolutely didn't intend to!"

"I have no idea what I said, can you tell me?"

The solution is to memorise your first 60 seconds so well, that if someone would wake you up in the middle of the night and ask: "What's your first 60 seconds?", you'd be able to tell it almost immediately. Memorising so thoroughly means that no matter how you feel or how your body reacts at the beginning of the pitch, you'll be able to deliver a successful opening.

With each sentence that you tell effectively, a signal is given to your instinct of being in control. It's as if you're sending messages saying: "Hey, we're not under attack. This is going fine, cut the adrenaline. No fight or flight required, please reconnect the brain!"

I've seen this work again and again. Let me give you an example.

Jim is a coder at a major consultancy. He was working on a blockchain innovation project and had been chosen to make a three-minute pitch in front of his big bosses.

181

He told me: "This is not my preferred place! I would rather be in front of my computer, coding!" Pitching was not his usual thing, and he was very nervous. Luckily, Jim took my 60-seconds advice very seriously. This is what he told me about giving his pitch:

"When I stood up, everything went white before my eyes. I could hardly see anything.

But then I started to deliver the opening of the pitch successfully. It was almost like the words were coming out of someone else's mouth! I felt like I was watching myself pitch and said to myself: "Hey, this is going pretty okay. Well done!"

After a couple of sentences, my focus began to kick in. Around 45 to 60 seconds into the pitch, I found myself feeling much more present and I started to get into the flow."

Put the work in to get the opening 60 seconds of your pitch absolutely rock solid, and you will have a solid platform for the rest of the pitch.

After the pitch, review how this helped you stay calm. It will help you build confidence for future pitches.

ACTION

Action – 30-minute task – Prepare the 60-second nerve buster.
1. Write out the first eight to nine sentences of your pitch. Include every word, even the simple parts such as: "Good evening, ladies and gentlemen."
2. Practice these words out loud, again and again, until you can remember them without looking at the script.

4.2.2 Amy Cuddy's science of body language to get rid of nerves

Amy Cuddy is a scientist with a fear of public speaking. In her TED Talk of 2012, she explained that your body posture can influence how you feel when preparing for moments of stress. The right body language can be a mental strengthener, but more importantly, it can even change the chemicals in your body in a way that helps boost your confidence.

Amy found that the body adjusts certain hormones when you stand for two minutes or more with your arms directly up in the air, like an Olympic runner's finish. Or with your hands on your hips, elbows and feet out, like Superwoman. During those two minutes, your body naturally starts creating additional testosterone, which is the power drug and reducing the production of cortisol, the stress drug.

More power and less stress means grace under pressure and a much higher chance of a successful pitch!

Through carrying out hundreds of experiments, Amy proved that over 90 percent of people perform better in stress situations when they follow these 'Power Pose' exercises of body posture. Doing them is the nearest thing to a guarantee of reducing your nerves.

However, there are situations where taking up a Power Pose might look a little nuts! Imagine that you are in a very small event with around 15 people. There are three other pitchers and you are the last to go. While waiting for your turn, you stand at the back with your arms up in the air and a big grin on your face, mouthing: "I feel great!" This might just make the others in the room think you've lost your marbles.

Luckily there's a way to translate Power Poses into an actionable approach for any pitch. Amy identified that they also work when sitting down. As you're waiting for your turn to pitch, sit with your head up, shoulders back and no arms or legs crossed. Do this for at least two minutes and you will also get a boost of testosterone and a decrease of cortisol. This will help bring you into the physical and mental state you need to make a great pitch.

4.2.3 Just breathe

In the minutes before you pitch, make sure you get some air into your lungs. It's another great tool you can use anytime, anywhere.

I've often heard pitchers say: "I felt as if the air was stuck in the top of my chest." Or: "I could hardly catch my breath." As a result, they found it hard to get their words out in a natural way and found themselves hurrying breathlessly through the pitch.

Take the time to breathe deeply: In through your nose, out through your mouth. This helps you become very present and ensures you will be able to breathe more easily when you start the pitch.

There is also some science behind it. By breathing deeply, you reduce your lev-els of cortisol. As mentioned, this is the stress drug. Breathing deeply therefore has an active and positive physical influence on reducing how agititated you feel.

It's a small but important element of preparing your mental and physical state to make a great pitch.

Just breathe.

Action – 10-minute task – Focus on your body posture and breathe consciously.

1. Before your next pitch, see if there is a place on site where you can try either of the two Power Poses. Ensure you hold a pose for at least two minutes.
2. If it's not possible to do a Power Pose without appearing strange, make sure you sit with good posture – head up, shoulders back, no legs or arms crossed – for at least two minutes.
3. In either case, breathe deeply in through your nose, out through your mouth, for those two minutes or more.

184

4.2.4 Get familiar with the location and equipment

Familiarity means less stress, which means you can reduce your pitching nerves by becoming familiar with the location. If you can check it out before the pitch, this will help you feel more comfortable and relaxed when you present. Here are a few things to look out for.

Is there a microphone? If yes, is it hand-held, or a headset? If there is no mic, will you need to speak a little louder than usual to reach everyone in the audience clearly?

Where is the screen situated and where can you stand? Make sure that you know where the projector light shines, so that you are not standing in the light.

Check the layout of the audience. How will you be sure to make contact with the whole audience? Will the letter W work in this set-up? (See page 162 for more on this.)

Is there a stage? If yes, can you move a little on stage and connect with people? Or is there a spotlight and might you wander off into the dark if you move?

Are you going to be introduced? If yes, where will you sit until that introduction? If there is a stage, make sure you've checked the steps up to it. I've seen plenty of people stumble as they enter the spotlight!

Is there a clicker or do you need to move from slide to slide manually on the computer? If there is a clicker, check the buttons in advance. Most have clarity on which button means forward, which button means back. Be sure you know for certain which is which.

And finally, don't forget to check the fonts and format of your presentation. There's nothing worse than presenting with your slides all messed up!

185

4.2.5 **Six more quick nerve-beating tips**

#1 Pause - then start

When you start your pitch, make sure you don't start speaking while walking onto the stage. Put half a second between the moment when you come to a stand-still, look at the audience and start.

This gives a clear signal to the audience that the pitch is about to start and it gives your brain a moment to engage with the content and make a confident opening.

#2 Avoid caffeine

Don't drink coffee or tea for at least two hours before the pitch. Both contain caffeine which increases your adrenaline.

Your adrenaline levels will already be a little higher than usual, and this extra caffeine spike may cause you to overheat, start to sweat and your heart may beat faster too. Stick to juices and water before the pitch, to ensure you're properly hydrated and relaxed when you start.

#3 No alcohol!

Yes, I mean it. If you ever get the advice to take a quick shot of alcohol before the big moment, please ignore that advice! It never works and can go seriously wrong. (I know, because I speak from bitter personal experience...)

I also recommend not to drink alcohol the night before a pitch, so that your mind is at its clearest at the big moment.

#4 Wear clothes that feel comfortable

If you don't usually wear a suit, it will feel very unnatural if you wear one for an important pitch. Choose a smart, comfortable jacket, a single-colour T-shirt, your best jeans and some clean shoes that fit well.

Equally, if wearing a suit makes you feel 'dressed for business' then go ahead and wear one. What matters most is to feel natural and comfortable.

#5 The audience is on your side

Believe it or not, the audience hopes that you will succeed. There is almost no-one who prefers to be in the spotlight compared to sitting in the audience, so they are happy it's you up there and not them!

#6 You don't look nervous!

The ratio to which you feel nervous, compared to how the audience perceives you, is always out of balance. I've often had someone deliver a solid, competent and confident test pitch in a workshop, and as soon as they finish, they blurt out: "Oh, I was really nervous! Did you see my knees knocking?"

How you feel is around five times as nervous as your audience can see.

Finally, doing the work ensures a reduction of nervousness.

Follow the process, tune in to your audience, be clear on your objective, get content down on Post-its®, test your opening sentences, boil it down to the Power of Three and film yourself from the first second to the last. All of this builds certainty, and will help you turn nerves into the energy you need to make a confident pitch that you are proud of.

INTERVIEW ROB VAN DEN HEUVEL

Client and CEO of SendCloud, the fastest growing startup in the Netherlands in 2017

Do you like pitching?

Honestly? I don't like pitching that much! I feel it's kind of bragging sometimes. That's not my thing. I'd rather be humbler, let people read about our company in other ways. But I recognise that it's a necessary thing for a startup and I'm okay with it now.

A few years ago, I would get very nervous although not so much these days. In the past I'd have been anxious two days before the pitch, now it's more like five minutes before!

What changed to calm down your nerves?

It's partly experience. You learn that nothing bad is really going to happen, right? Even if you screw up – which I obviously did once or twice at Startupbootcamp! – it's not the end of the world. You learn and it's good experience. On the other hand, the company grows and as you get bigger, pitching becomes more of a talk about real achievements and products that have value, not just hopes and ideas.

You were the fastest growing startup in the Netherlands last year, with some millions in yearly revenue. Do you still have to pitch?

Yes, but less to investors and more to customers. Recently, we started the process of integrating with one of the largest online marketplaces in the Benelux. I had to pitch there to convince them to work with our tool and that was a big one. Now I'm mainly pitching to a smaller group instead of events like Demo Days and competitions in front of hundreds of people. If it's for an audience, it's more about telling your story, not the selling or investment pitch anymore.

Think back to the early days: You've given a successful Demo Day pitch and now you have a one-hour meeting at an investor's office. What's it like to pitch in that situation?

You prepare a pitch like always and they ask you to go through your pitch deck. It's usually a maximum of 10 minutes presentation and the rest is questions, often to shoot holes in your business plan! And even in the presentation they will jump in and ask. Pitch... boom, question! Continue to pitch and boom, question again! They want to test you, face to face, and see how you react, because they know customers will do the same.

What's your biggest advice to other founders, starting on the journey to pitch for investment?

You'll be nervous, but just do it and prepare. I used to be the worst guy at preparing, but the more you do the work in advance, the less nervous you are. You know what you're going to say, you know your story, the facts, and all that preparation work means you become less anxious. In the first year, my co-founder Sabi and I used to go to a bar downstairs and take a shot of whisky! We don't do that anymore and I'm not sure if I would recommend it...

As you grow, do others in your team need to be lead pitchers?

At customer-centric events, like the Magento Conference or E-Commerce Day, my sales leaders pitch. Still, for the big events, usually they want to hear from the CEO. Gradually though, we're giving more people in the team the opportunity to pitch and some of them really like it. If they do like it, I'm delighted: Sure, go ahead! Sometimes it goes wrong – they tell the wrong story, or focus on the wrong things – but okay. Again, nothing bad happens and they learn.

One last comment about pitching?

Just do it. Go for it and if you fail, do it again! I used to be quite a shy person and learning to pitch and doing it regularly certainly helped me get through that. ●

189

OH... ONE MORE THING

The one single thread I've noticed when asking for advice from anyone who listens to pitches is this: They all say:

"Passion and enthusiasm count."

My goal with this book is to ensure you are professional, well organised and clear with your message. I've also shared ways to keep the story natural. Reading it out loud, identifying the words that change the meaning and keeping connected with the content.

Often it is the feeling as much as the content that triggers someone to follow-up after the pitch. The more you feel like you are telling your own story and not the one you feel you should tell, the better chance you have of resonating with your audience and finding the people who can help you grow your ideas into a business and beyond.

**Be Professional. Be Passionate.
And Pitch to Win!**

TO WRAP IT UP

You've come on a great journey while developing your pitching skills. Ideally, you've had a chance to test the tools and feel the results of this new way of pitching. Script, Design and Deliver is now working for you!

My last advice is to keep going. Pitch wherever and whenever you get the chance, and stick to the process you've followed throughout this book.

If you find yourself launching into slide software before the story is clear, force yourself to find the Post-its® and the Pitch Canvas© to get your story straight first. Whenever you realise you forgot to make a profile of the audience, push yourself to go back, review who they are and what they care about. And if you're beginning to get nervous again, do the work to master those first 60 seconds!

Perhaps most important of all: Teach others on your team to become great pitchers. Work through the exercises with them and share your own experiences of learning these new tools. Inspire them to raise their game too. It's a great asset to have one outstanding pitcher in the team, it's an even greater asset to have a few!

I wish you the maximum success by using these tools to get the results you need to grow to the next level. Good luck with your next pitch and every pitch in the future!

THANK YOU

Big and heartfelt Thank Yous go to;

Sheila, for investing in, believing in and supporting me to build this business together – and for giving me the platform to find my passion. Without you, a lot fewer great ideas would have a voice.

Robin Dohmen, for great work on many projects and pitches, and for being the main influencer for the Design section of this book. You are the best slide designer I have ever met and it's a pleasure to work with you.

Michael Dooijes, for constant support, belief, and offering me a lifeline when I needed it most. You are constantly doing what it takes and your never-ending energy is an inspiration to many.

Patrick and Ruud at Startupbootcamp, you gave me the platform to learn and develop the Pitch to Win methodology. (It's been a long journey since coffee at Hanneke's Boom!)

Lance Miller, who started it all back in 1992. You taught me that if they want a sheet of A4, give them a document. If they want a document, give them a presentation. If they want a presentation, give them the best pitch they have ever seen.

Would you like your pitch to be featured in a future edition of this book or on our website?

If you've used the tools in this book to create your pitch, and feel others could learn from the way you have Scripted, Designed and Delivered it, feel free to share it with us.

To be considered, send us three things:
- The final script, in any standard text format.
- The slides as a pdf file.
- A reasonable quality movie of you delivering the pitch.

Send us all three plus your contact details by WeTransfer to pitch@best3minutes.com

Please note that only pitches with all three elements (script, slides and movie) will be considered, and that by sending us the files you agree to us sharing them online and in print, for commercial use.

ABOUT THE AUTHOR

David Beckett has coached over 700 startups to win over €170 million in investments. He has also trained thousands of professionals in innovation teams at companies such as Google, IKEA, Booking.com, ING, Unilever and PwC, to pitch to the Board for resources for their game-changing innovation projects. He's a TEDx speech coach at TEDx Amsterdam, CERN and Munich.

David Beckett provides active and inspiring Keynote talks to large and medium-sized events and congresses.

See him in action and find out more at best3minutes.com/keynote-speaker. Contact him for bookings at speaker@best3minutes.com.

David also delivers interactive and transformative training for Accelerators, Corporate Innovation programs and major companies. Contact Best3minutes for more information at info@best3minutes.com.

197

BE PROFESSIONAL.
BE PASSIONATE.
AND PITCH TO WIN!

Printed in Great Britain
by Amazon